Labor Intermediation Services in Developing Economies

Jacqueline Mazza

Labor Intermediation Services in Developing Economies

Adapting Employment Services for a Global Age

palgrave
macmillan

Jacqueline Mazza
Johns Hopkins University
School of Advanced International Studies
Washington, DC, USA

ISBN 978-1-137-48667-7   ISBN 978-1-137-48668-4   (eBook)
DOI 10.1057/978-1-137-48668-4

Library of Congress Control Number: 2016959411

Cover image © Zero Creatives / Getty

Printed on acid-free paper

This Palgrave Macmillan imprint is published by Springer Nature
The registered company is Springer International Publishing AG
The registered company address is: Gewerbestrasse 11, 6330 Cham, Switzerland

For my son Daniel

PREFACE

In 1904 in urban Philadelphia, USA, William Rees, a weaver, walked from employer to employer, sometimes four miles a day to find work.[1] More than 100 years later, throughout the developing world, such informal, inefficient ways to find low-paid work remain. Today in Mexico City, if you need a plumber you can still stroll to the Zocalo, Mexico's ancient Aztec plaza, and find an aging plumber sitting in front of a cardboard box marked "*plomero*."

Spanning the industrial to post-industrial age, the United States and the now developed nations grew extensive and diffuse markets that connect job seekers with work and the skills to get work. Wandering grew to newspaper want ads to employment services offices to today all of the above – internet-based job services, walk-in employment service centers, graduate schools placing their students, recruitment agencies and personal contacts. Economists would call this a "market" between buyers and sellers of labor services, working imperfectly but much better than in developing economies.

Developing economies in the 21st century are more informal, have greater poverty, and share market and migration routes with highly advanced economies using electronic networks – a complexity unimaginable to William Rees walking the streets of Philadelphia only 100 years ago. But too often in developing countries traces of a vibrant job search market are hard to find, particularly for the world's poor. The majority of the poor in the developing world find work through other poor friends and family – and guess what? They find other precarious, dead-end jobs, or invent ones most cannot imagine, such as seller of empty milk containers (rural Tanzania), garbage picker (India), or fire eater at a traffic stop (Mexico).

This book is for developing countries and policy practitioners who do not have the luxury of a century of development to create more formal markets to help workers find better work. It is the product of 20 years of practical experience trying to help build labor services to combat the chaotic, elite-biased ways of finding work in the developing world, principally in Latin America and the Caribbean, but now for other developing economies. It is a book about how developing countries can and are already improving how people get jobs. It is a book with developing country examples at every turn. These countries started with what the developed world calls "employment services" but they quickly learned that the limitations of public financing, informal economies and poor job creation would never sustain the employment services models of the developed countries. What this book lays out are stages to building from basic employment services to a more country-specific set of "labor intermediation services" that better fit the institutional and market challenges of developing economies in a more global world.

Your indulgence is requested in my using the term "developing countries" to represent a broad spectrum of countries from low-income economies to former transition economies to high-income Middle Eastern countries to emerging economies that have graduated to OECD membership, such as Korea and Chile. The term "developing countries" is used as an inaccurate shorthand but with the goal of drawing common lessons across developing and now highly developed economies, even if many have now leaped out of the developing category.

Economists widely – and rightly – argue that the key problem in developing economies is not finding a good job, it's that enough good jobs aren't there. No argument there. This book is not a fight with those economists. Rather it is to show what 20 years of practical experience have taught me. That by small investments in basic employment services – the easiest and actually most cost-effective active labor market policy – one can stimulate and support the growth of a wider range of labor intermediation services that can play a role in providing better market signals to schools, training institutions and private firms. It is one piece, not a panacea, for fixing the jobs quagmire in the developing world. The last chapter discusses a bit more how intermediation can be integrated within larger jobs and human capital efforts.

The next age of development is coming around to a more conscious focus on employment as the most promising route out of poverty or, as recently put, "development happens through jobs." In doing so, better labor intermediation services will have a role to play but we have to think differently about them and their connections with education, training, skills and economic growth.

This book would not be possible without the open doors of Labor Ministries, national employment services, NGO specialists, private sector leaders and dedicated professionals who have enabled me to watch, shape and learn what is working in very different developing country economies. I particularly thank colleagues at the Inter-American Development Bank where I worked for over 15 years, the World Bank, and International Labour Organization who helped me learn while doing. Sabina Viera Almeida da Silva and Caitlyn McCrone of the Johns Hopkins University, School of Advanced International Studies (SAIS) provided excellent research support. I dedicate this book to my college son Daniel who already sees the world more connected than I. His sage advice was: don't make this book "too boring." Well, let's see.

NOTE

1. As cited in Joshua Rosenbloom, <u>Looking for Work, Searching for Workers,</u> 2002, p. xiii.

Johns Hopkins University   Jacqueline Mazza
School of Advanced International Studies
Washington, DC, USA

CONTENTS

1   Jobs and Job Search in Developing Countries:
    Nice Work if You Can Get it!   1

2   Employment and Labor Intermediation Services:
    What Are They and What Are They Good For?   19

3   Stage 1: Building Core Employment Services   39

4   Stage 2: From Employment to Labor Intermediation
    Services   65

5   A Stage 3? Labor Intermediation and the New Jobs
    Agenda for Development   113

Bibliography   137

Index   145

LIST OF FIGURES AND BOXES

Graph 1.1	"Friends and Family" – dominant job search method in Latin America	4
Graph 1.2	Informal job search greater for the less educated	5
Graph 1.3	Employer difficulty in filling skilled jobs, 2015	14
Graph 3.1	Proportion of individuals with internet access by region	50
Graph 4.1	Growth in individuals using the internet by income classification	90
Box 3.1	Seven Years in Honduras: A Stage 1 Public-Private Launchpad for Jobs	44
Box 3.2	Neighbor-to-Neighbor: Advancing a Regional Technical Support Network in Employment Services	55
Box 3.3	Growing from Crisis Mode: South Korea's Rapid Transition out of Stage 1	61
Box 4.1	Building Life and Job Skills in Poor Neighborhoods: Youth Build goes International and to South Africa	77
Box 5.1	Riviera Maya, Mexico: Strategic Growth in Tourism, Integrating from the Right and Center	121
Box 5.2	Hungary: Advancing a Career-Development/Guidance System in a Skills-Driven Economy	133

LIST OF TABLES

Table 1.1   Vulnerable employment by key country and income category   9
Table 1.2   Emigration and immigration rates – developing countries   11
Table 2.1   Service types – core functions versus extended services   26
Table 2.2   Tailoring active labor market programs to labor market needs   34
Table 4.1   Extended service types   70
Table 4.2   A snapshot of public-private intermediation markets:
            Middle East and North Africa   104
Table 5.1   Diverse job challenges; diverse jobs strategies:
            Perspectives from the World Development Report   116

CHAPTER 1

Jobs and Job Search in Developing Countries: Nice Work if You Can Get it!

Jobs often do not get the attention they deserve in development, one scholar calling this lack of attention "jobs dementia." Quite simply, getting and keeping a decent-wage job has been found to be the most important factor in enabling the poor to get out of poverty and stay out.[1] It is also the single most important factor to explain the decline of inequality in those countries that have seen a decline. This makes sense even without a lot of econometric studies when we remember that the poor have only their labor – no financial assets – with which to exit poverty permanently.

There are many policies and programs that need to interact well together to increase the ability of all, but particularly of the poor (who comprise nearly half the developing world, earning two dollars or less a day) to get, keep or move into a good paying job. So many in the developing world earn meager wages for time-consuming but low productivity work; thus, improving both the job and the fit of the worker to the job is part of advancing labor productivity and employment that, in turn, feeds economic growth.

This book is about one (but not all) of the policies needed for better employment. It is about developing services that connect those looking for jobs with a job they likely would not have known about or been considered for on their own. The "active labor market" policy used in advanced countries is termed "employment services." Employment services date back to WWI and have traditionally been run by the public

© The Author(s) 2017
J. Mazza, *Labor Intermediation Services in Developing Economies*,
DOI 10.1057/978-1-137-48668-4_1

sector, but everywhere in the world their form and their associated partnerships are evolving with the changing global labor market. The economic rationale for employment services remains largely the same though, they aim to help more people get better jobs faster – less time searching for work, less time unemployed, a better fit in the job, leading to less job rotation, and better income over time. In the most advanced countries, both public and private employment services have evolved simultaneously into a combination of public, private, online, and in-person services that openly list jobs and help with the match between employer and job seeker. In the developed countries, think Manpower Group, Monster.com, together with your local job board, your school, and friends of your uncle in the business.

This chapter will lay out some of the foundations of job search in developing countries, looking first at a variety of evidence and studies that demonstrate what one may already have guessed – that finding even an existing job in developing economies is relatively difficult and that the poor are particularly disadvantaged. The second section tries to broaden the understanding of who might be looking for work in developing countries and then places job search in the context of the bigger, lack-of-good-jobs problem. It is hard to estimate the potential employment and productivity gains just from improving job matching and getting more jobs more openly listed. However, this book argues it is worthwhile to think of one gain further, as many associated labor market mismatches are indirectly affected by the lack of knowledge about labor market demand and the poor functioning of the institutions preparing the workforce. Acknowledging all along the way the great dysfunctions in the labor markets of most developing countries, the chapters that follow lay out how the basic employment service model should be adapted differently to fit the markets of developing countries. This introductory chapter sets up the rest of the book taking a look at how poorly job search currently operates in most developing countries as well as at the bigger jobs "problem" – informality, poor quality jobs, skills mismatches, and more – hence, the subtitle: "nice work if you can get it!"

Searching for Jobs in Developing Countries

Job search in most developing countries is rarely possible for the vast majority of the labor force in the modern form that it takes in developed economies. First, very few jobs are openly listed or openly competed for in the developing world. The problem is not just that employers are reluctant to list openings or that information is not available – what we can call market failures due to a lack of transparency and lack of information. It is also that job hiring is inefficient, time-consuming and unfair in most of the developing world, including involving the elite hiring of friends of friends and the more educated waiting for poor quality public sector jobs. Productivity is brought down, both by the poor match of the worker to the actual job and the time spent moving between low productivity jobs.

Limited to Non-existent Open Job Listings

There is typically no consistent information on just how few jobs are openly listed and fairly competed for in the developing world. We know it is small, even more so in countries with little formal employment. Employers will say they don't have time to list openings, and if they do, they will get a flood of applicants outside their doors (true, for sure). Limited public listings are part of a bigger information "market failure" where it's hard to look for jobs when you don't know who is hiring and what fields are growing. The dimension of the information and intermediation problem in developing countries is varied, but even in countries where there is no job growth there is job rotation. This lack of an open market has fueled what is often a highly uncompetitive and even politicized culture of hiring.

Whether openly listed or not, economists often talk about formal versus informal methods of job search. Formal methods have concrete institutions attached to them – applying for an advertised opening, using a public or private employment service, or the internet. Informal methods are just that, relational and unsystematic – asking a friend, relative or work associate about jobs, stopping by a firm without knowing if there are any openings. One is not necessarily more effective than the other; in fact, most studies show multiple job search methods usually get better results faster. What matters is what method works best for a person with a particular profile, how long it takes, and whether formal or informal methods result in getting a better job. It is generally observed in developed countries that the unemployed are more likely to use formal methods (often a requirement of getting their unemployment insurance checks) while people currently working use informal methods more. But what about in developing countries?

"Friends and Family": The Dominant Job Search Method in Developing Countries: ... Works Well Only with the Right Friends and Family

Developing countries with very different kinds of job markets vary in how much formal or informal search methods are used, although informal methods usually dominate, particularly in countries where most of the jobs are informal. In Latin America and the Caribbean, we know informal job search dominates every country (Graph 1.1). For emerging and developing countries, we know about job search methods only if the labor force is asked this question regularly in a labor force survey. "Friends" is also the overwhelming response in the Middle East and North Africa when workers are asked how they found a job – from over 70% in Lebanon, over 60% in Syria (2010), and over 30% in Yemen and Egypt.[2]

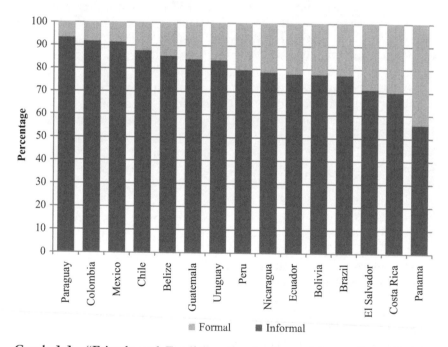

Graph 1.1 "Friends and Family" – the dominant job search method in Latin America

(Source: Calculations from annual labor force surveys, various years 2007–2010. Jacqueline Mazza, *Fast Tracking Jobs: Advances and Next Steps in Labor Intermediation Services in Latin America and the Caribbean*, Inter-American Development Bank, Washington, DC, 2011.)

As Graph 1.1 shows, the proportion of informal search in Latin America and the Caribbean can vary greatly from just over 50% in a growing, middle-income country like Panama with comparatively better secondary education to more than 90% in Paraguay, a country where most employment is informal and poverty is comparatively high. Despite higher formality and income, informal job search still dominates in middle-income developing countries like Colombia (92%) and Mexico (91%). The efficiency and effectiveness of using informal "friends and family" to find work depends on how good those contacts are – and here is the core problem for the poor in developing countries. The poor know only other poor who have low-wage or survival employment, hence a few more fire eaters and garbage pickers. When a poor nurse in Nigeria just recently lost her job, she turned not to looking for a job in another clinic but to selling peanuts where she had immediate contacts.[3]

It is the less educated overall who rely disproportionately on informal job search and have the contacts for poorer jobs. Survey data for Latin America and the Caribbean shown in Graph 1.2 confirms that those with

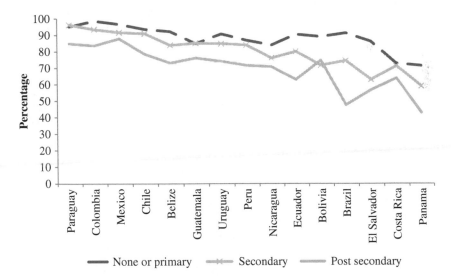

Graph 1.2 Informal job search greater for the less educated (percent of informal job search by level of education)
(Source: Calculations from annual labor force surveys, various years 2007–2010. Jacqueline Mazza, *Fast Tracking Jobs: Advances and Next Steps in Labor Intermediation Services in Latin America and the Caribbean*, Inter-American Development Bank, Washington, DC, 2011.)

primary education or less used informal job search the most, across developing countries of varied income levels.

Garcia and Nicodermo found that it is not just "friends and family" that matters for informal job search, but neighborhoods (a wider circle of friends).[4] What did they find for the difference between those who lived in poor neighborhoods versus wealthier neighborhoods? They found using data from Colombia that the chances of finding a job – whether by informal or formal methods – increased depending on how your neighborhood looks for work. People tended to use the methods most used by other employed people in the neighborhood, and workers referred to job opportunities in poor neighborhoods earned less due to the nature of their contacts.[5] Job search methods and contacts reinforced existing income inequality with strong "informational asymmetries" depending on where you lived.

Informal job search has another disadvantage for those already in the informal sector – it has also been found to increase the probability that you will find informal, low quality work. Gustavo Marquez and Cristobal Ruiz-Tagle found in Venezuela that workers coming from the formal sector were more likely to use formal methods, and informal workers or the self-employed, informal methods.[6] Marquez and Ruiz-Tagle's study found that it was this informal or formal labor market history – more than education, age or gender – that determined the search strategy.[7] They found that it was the use of formal employment agencies – regardless of labor market history – that was the most effective in getting a job, followed second by informal methods and last by use of the media. Research from Great Britain similarly confirmed that it was low-skilled workers and the long-term unemployed – those with poor contacts – who benefitted the most from a formal public employment service.[8]

The "friends and family" model in the developing world also reinforces discriminatory practices well beyond economic, education and work status, reinforcing gender, ethnic and cultural stereotypes that keep people from being considered for more productive and more formal jobs. Women and indigenous groups are more likely to have even poorer job contacts. In a literature review of developing countries, a job search advantage for men was found in having a wider range of more work-centered networks.[9] Even in using formal methods, women, ethnic groups, and castes as in India were referred to jobs that the referrer considered culturally appropriate, reinforcing severe occupational segregation and low pay levels. A labor market survey of Bolivia, a country where there is a majority of indigenous peoples, found that women work in jobs with less socio-economic status and more domestic responsibilities; this constrained their ability to create the social networks and channels needed to find salaried employment.[10] In many Middle Eastern and African countries, political parties, tribes are among the distinct social groups that can control distinct government ministries and private firms making employment more of a patronage system, institutionalizing discrimination.

Job Seekers in Developing Countries: The Hidden, the Discouraged, and the Mobile

If we are to improve job search in developing countries, we need to consider how different are the groups of job seekers and the labor market conditions they face within an increasingly diverse developing world. In developing economies, the potential size of the "intermediation" problem – or the improvement in the labor market one can get by opening up employment listings and just matching workers more quickly to better jobs – is clearly limited by the availability of jobs themselves. It is also limited because the client may have different job search horizons (migration) or may be discouraged, disconnected, without the right skills, or trapped in survival employment and thus not actively looking.

Employment services in the industrialized countries began by targeting officially unemployed adults displaced from manufacturing jobs. Only over time did they begin serving new entrants and the services sector. In developing and middle-income market economies, the client base for employment-intermediation services has to be thought of as comprising both official and hidden job seekers, if the latter had the right services and support. This second section reviews some of these very different "potential" clients of employment, growing into labor, intermediation, services – building first from the officially unemployed, a smaller group in many developing countries, but extending to the poorly employed, the discouraged, and the mobile. The intention here is to be illustrative, not comprehensive. With apologies for over generalization and omission, here are some of the diverse sets of would-be job hunters in developing countries that each have very different needs for job search. Let's take a look at some of these very diverse kinds of potential job seekers:

The Un, Under and Poorly Employed

The very high rates of adult unemployment heard of in Greece, Italy, and Spain, for example, are considered a luxury in the developing world. Though there are only a few developing countries where official adult unemployment rates are over 20%, such as the countries of Sub-Saharan Africa (e.g. South Africa, Namibia), Western Africa (e.g. Mauritania) and Surinam,[11] youth unemployment, always higher than adult unemployment, can be particularly severe in certain developing regions – the Middle East and Sub-Saharan Africa of note. The Middle East and North Africa face both high rates of youth unemployment and high birth rates, termed a youth "bulge." Youth unemployment (15–24 ages) is over 50% in South Africa, Croatia, and Bulgaria, over 31% in the Middle East and North Africa and 28% in the small states of the Caribbean (2013).[12] We do know that being unemployed early in your career or having a precarious set of first jobs with periods of non-activity has long-term implications on earnings.

What is a more universal jobs problem throughout both developing and emerging market countries is what economist Gary Fields calls "working hard, working poor."[13] This refers to the vast numbers of low-income workers, working extremely long hours but in often informal jobs where they earn very little. These are the workers who fit the bill of wanting better work if it was available or accessible – "nice work if you can get it". Informal work is typically defined as work without benefits, a formal contract or security. Individual street sellers, coffee pickers and traders typically come to mind, but this group also includes workers in firms that are themselves informal, that is, the boss doesn't pay taxes or formally register the business. Waged and salaried employment is growing globally, albeit slowly; it dominates Central and South-East Europe, Russia and the members of the CIS, where eight out of ten workers are employees, but the reverse is the case in South Asia and Sub-Saharan Africa where only two out of ten workers are salaried.[14] In the case of Kenya, only 1.3 million work in the formal modern sector and 12 million in the informal sector, nearly half that number in smallholder farming.[15] Due to such different national definitions, informality is often hard to commonly measure across regions of the world. The International Labour Organization (ILO) calculates that around half the world's workers are in vulnerable employment.[16] These are defined as own-account workers and ones contributing to family employment; these are predominantly women, with jobs and

Table 1.1 Vulnerable employment by key country and income category (as % of total employment)

High income		Upper middle income		Lower middle income		Low income	
Norway	5.3%	Brazil	23.1%	Egypt	26.3%	Ethiopia	88.8%
Germany	6.3%	Turkey	29.3%	Philippines	38.4%	Uganda	78.9%

Source: "Vulnerable Employment as a % of Total Employment: 2013" in World Bank, Labor Market Indicators. Accessed on January 23, 2016.

income that are precarious and at survival levels. Table 1.1 shows the differences in vulnerable employment across different countries in different income categories. The ILO reports higher rates and volumes of vulnerable employment in South Asia and Sub-Saharan Africa. Higher rates of vulnerability, e.g. poorer quality employment, is most severe in the lower-income developing countries such as Ethiopia and Uganda (Table 1.1) where less than 20% of employment is not in this category.

With wide differences in countries noted, the unemployed are more typically just a subset of much larger swaths of poor workers, moving in and out of, or stuck in, vulnerable or survival employment who might benefit from a more competitive and functional labor market. Not counted in this group is a growing phenomenon of those not looking at all, the discouraged, particularly youth.

The Discouraged, the Idle: Neither Working, Studying, Training Nor Searching for Work

Many of the potential beneficiaries in better job matching may be hidden in developing countries or staying out of the labor market for other reasons. This goes well beyond the label of "discouraged" workers the term given in the advanced countries for those who have stopped looking when there are very few jobs, as during the height of the 2009–10 financial crisis. More than voluntarily discouraged, women's labor force participation varies markedly around the globe, and is particularly constrained culturally in the Middle East and North Africa.

Of particular recent concern has been the young in the developing world, particularly the rise of those who appear in statistics to be neither working, nor studying, nor in training nor searching for work. It even has a statistical name – NEET – neither in education, employment or training. Labor force participation for youth is down everywhere in the world apart from Sub-Saharan Africa. It is particularly low in the Middle East (31%) and North Africa (34%), but dropped 20 points in the last 25 years in East Asia to 55%.[17] In many cases, particularly in East Asia, youth in education are thus not working which is a good sign for the future labor market. Others may be in caretaker roles, particularly women; while others are ill or disabled. But the phenomenon has grown and cannot be easily explained by these factors. It has taken on different regional dimensions with concerns about the growing "idleness" of youth or their potential participation in illicit drug trades. In higher-income families, particularly in the high-income countries of the Middle East, these can include young people discouraged from the job market who can afford to live at home but are angry about it, or women raising families where both their home work and their labor market participation has limited value. Labor force participation for young women in the Middle East was only 13.8% in 2014, compared to over 50% in East Asia and Sub-Saharan Africa.[18] Global concern was so united that substantially reducing the number of young people neither in education, training or employment was made a target of the 2030 Sustainable Development Goals (target 6.5).

The Mobile: Economic Migrants

Migrating to find work, or work one can live on, is a dominant feature of most developing economies, whether migrating within or across countries. Mexico to the USA, Ukraine to the Russian Federation (and vice versa), Bangladesh to India may be the most famous and largest migration corridors, but migration is changing labor markets within and across developing countries more and more – Bangladeshis selling goods in India, Hondurans working the fields in El Salvador, Philippine maids in Saudi Arabia. In high-income developing countries in the Middle East, migrants are the *majority* of the labor force, and dominate low-skilled work. In some small nations, outmigration, particularly of the well educated, is startlingly high – West Bank and Gaza (68%), Guyana (57%), Albania (45%).[19]

The figures presented in Table 1.2 are intended to underscore why migration support services are or should be part of a mix of services to support employment in key developing countries.[20] Table 1.2 presents migration in developing countries by number of persons within a country (stock) and rates as a percentage of the population – both for those leaving (emigration) and those coming in (immigration).

Table 1.2 Emigration and immigration rates – developing countries (total stock and % of population)

Region	Emigration		Immigration	
	Stock (in 1000s)	% of population	Stock (in 1000s)	% of population
East Asia and Pacific	21.7 million	1.1	5.4 million	0.3
China	8,343.6	0.6	685.8	0.1
Philippines	4,275.2	4.6	435.4	0.5
Indonesia	2,502.3	1.1	122.9	0.1
Europe and Central Asia	43.1 million	10.7	27.3 million	6.8
The Russian Federation	11,055.6	7.9	12,270.4	8.7
Ukraine	6,563.1	14.4	5,257.5	11.6
Turkey	4,261.6	5.6	1,410.9	1.9
Kazakhstan	3,717.3	23.6	3,079.5	19.5
Latin America and the Caribbean	30.2 million	5.2	6.6 million	1.1
Mexico	11,859.2	10.7	725.7	0.7
El Salvador	1,269.1	20.5	40.3	0.7
Costa Rica	125.3	2.7	489.2	10.5
Middle East and North Africa	18.1 million	5.3	12.0 million	3.5
West Bank and Gaza	3,013.7	68.3	1,923.8	43.6
Jordan	733.6	11.3	2,973.0	45.9
Lebanon	664.1	15.6	758.2	17.8
South Asia	26.7 million	1.6	12.2 million	0.7
India	11,357.5	0.9	5,436.0	0.4
Bangladesh	5,380.2	3.3	1,085.3	0.7
Sri Lanka	1,847.5	9.1	339.9	1.7
Sub-Saharan Africa	21.8 million	2.5	17.7 million	2.1
Burkina Faso	1,576.4	9.7	1,043.0	6.4
Zimbabwe	1,253.1	9.9	372.3	2.9
Mozambique	1,178.5	5.0	450.0	1.9

Source: Migration and Remittances Factbook, World Bank 2011.

International migration data cannot keep pace with current flows. This World Bank data indicates that the highest emigration rates in both numbers and on a percentage basis are in Europe and Central Asia, but then Chinese migration follows in large volumes but particularly to the East Asia region, but this is much smaller as a percentage of the population (1.1%). Some of the countries with the largest emigration rates, such as the West Bank and Gaza largely to Israel, represent relatively small populations on a global scale, but significant ones to local economies.

Although foreign workers comprise significant segments of many developing and high-income economies, in only a few nations are these workers deemed eligible for and permitted access to information and services for better jobs and improving their human capital. Even internal mobility, information and support for workers to move from job-poor to job-rich areas are subject to constraints in countries such as China and those formerly associated with the Soviet Union. Chapter 4 will lay out more specific ways in which migration support services have been used in different developing countries to make migration safer, associated with better information, and occasionally more human capital-enhancing for economic migrants.

The Bigger Job Context: The Low Job Quality, Skills Mismatch, Low Productivity, Low Job Creation Vortex

We cannot conclude this chapter on understanding job search and diverse job seekers in developing countries without acknowledging the obvious. Wouldn't this all be a small transactional and informational problem if there were just enough good quality jobs in home countries? All developing countries, and many developed economies, face both a labor demand problem – too few, poor quality and low productivity jobs – and a supply problem – poorly prepared and poorly educated workforces to fit the demand. The demand and supply problems, and they are multiple, are not resolved by any one intervention, but they do put a limitation on any modest gains that can be made by improving and expanding the job-matching process.

These supply and demand constraints take on very different national characteristics based on differences in population cohorts (youth bulge, aging population), education systems (skills development, relevance to employment), and economic growth patterns, to name but a few. This has led international institutions and donors to work on jobs "strategies" for individual countries, one-employment-size-fits-all now officially banished. Good job matches, however, cannot work well when workers have poor or the wrong skills (labor supply problems) or there are not enough or the wrong kind of jobs (labor demand problems). As will be clearer

in subsequent chapters, labor intermediation services can play a supporting role in addressing the range of disconnections (e.g. skills, economic
growth, education) that may contribute to the problem. Just a quick,
admittedly too superficial, look down into the vortex into some labor supply and demand constraints.

Supply Mismatches: Worker Skills/Qualifications versus What Employers Need

It is not just that job contacts are poor and job search methods may be
inefficient, biased against key groups, or non-existent. A key and growing
problem is that available jobs go unfilled or are filled by those who may
not have the basic skills or qualifications. In short, employers are looking
for workers with certain skills and can't find them. Employers don't have
the right supply of job seekers to fit current demand, let alone sufficient
confidence in the labor force to make investments in better jobs for future
growth. This is often called a skills-mismatch problem, or as Manpower
Group calls it, a "talent shortage."

Manpower Group, an international private placement firm, surveys
employers worldwide each year, asking whether they are having difficulty
filling jobs and, if so, which jobs. The skills-mismatch problem is clearly not
confined to developing countries. Rather, it is more country-specific and it is
on the rise. In 2015, the countries where employers reported the most difficulty in filling jobs were Japan (83%), Peru (68%) and Hong Kong (65%).[21]
Graph 1.3 shows that more developing and middle-income countries exceed
the global average (35% in 2015) than fall below, but that this pattern is
not consistent when countries are grouped by income level.[22] A region like
Central and Eastern Europe is equally divided between economies where
employers find comparatively large skill shortages (Bulgaria, Romania)
and those well below the global average (Slovakia, Czech Republic).

A skills mismatch has many roots, from education and training institutions not producing sufficient numbers or sufficiently qualified graduates
in the fields where jobs are, to perverse incentives, misinformation or cultural stereotypes prompting job seekers to get skilled in areas where there
is little work. A problem noted in the Middle East is that highly educated
young people stay out of the labor market for years preparing for and
awaiting public sector jobs for the sake of prestige and security, despite the
dwindling number and value of these positions. While Graph 1.3 shows

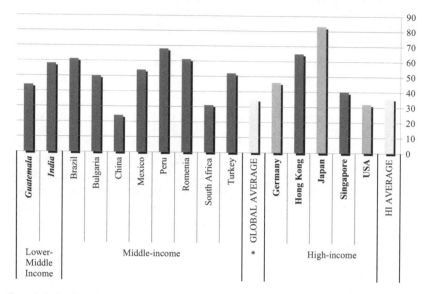

Graph 1.3   Employer difficulty in filling skilled jobs (% of surveyed employers) (Source: *2015 Talent Shortage Survey*, Manpower Group, 2015. Regional classifications based on World Bank Country Classification by Income, 2016 Fiscal Year, July 2015.)

the skills-mismatch problem is large throughout the world, it is the *consequences* that may be greater for developing countries. Many of the lowest-income countries were not surveyed, but South Africa demonstrates how mid-sized skill mismatches can exist simultaneously in low-income countries with high unemployment (31% of employers with difficulty finding skilled workers even with unemployment rates of 50%).[23] The institutional and informational gaps feeding the skills mismatch can occur all along the skills spectrum. Even though it is relatively low-skilled work, Manpower Group found that drivers moved up to a high position among the jobs that were hard for employers to fill. Despite job growth Southeast Asia has a diverse range of jobs "problems." Indonesia's "jobs problem" has been determined to be more a poor job creation problem as so much employment (44%) is in low productivity agriculture. Nearly half of all Indonesian firms in a recent USAID review had vacancies for professional and skilled workers, but this figure was still lower than in nearby Thailand and Bangladesh where 70% of firms couldn't find professional workers and

80% couldn't find the skilled workers they needed.[24] To be fair, services to match workers to jobs which include labor market information systems cannot in themselves fix a skills mismatch in a given country, but they can play a role in improving the labor market information and market signaling needed to reduce the mismatch.

Demand Constraints: Lousy Work ... If You Can Get It

The good or decent jobs deficit is no stranger to developing economies. Despite tremendous progress in poverty reduction and remarkable productivity-led growth in Asia, too many workers are still working in lousy jobs. "Lousy" should include jobs at poverty wages, vulnerable employment (Table 1.1), jobs offering few prospects for career and skill development, as well as informal employment without benefits. The ILO estimates 28% of workers in developing countries are working poor, earning less than $2 a day, while another 25% are working near poor, earning $2–$4 a day.[25] The percentage of poor workers has been dropping dramatically, particularly in China and South Asia, and was nearly double today's rates at 68% of all workers in 1991.[26] The quality and nature of the job matters in terms of salary and well-being and thus poverty reduction. Among both developed and developing countries, Hungary and Bulgaria saw particularly large increases in households in poverty from the 2000s – over 10% – explained just by more households moving to interim, temporary or part-time employment.[27]

Increasing economic growth is a dominant but not the sole factor in better job creation. Employment worldwide has yet to recover from the global financial crisis; the ILO estimates there is still a jobs "deficit" of 61 million compared with 2007 levels.[28] While employment levels seem to be recovering in a number of developed economies, though not in Europe, key countries in the developing world after some impressive pre-crisis growth are still sluggish both in employment and economic growth, most notably China, Latin America, and Asia. Labor productivity growth, measured in terms of output per worker, is needed to spur good job growth. However, labor productivity can be double-edged in terms of jobs impacts, efficiency gained in one area sometimes being at the expense of fewer jobs unless it is also accompanied by economic growth. Productivity growth has been slowing in the developed world, particularly in Japan, and it is near zero in Russia. Developing countries have been affected by the slowdown in China's productivity growth, which at 7% in 2015 is down from 9% but still enviable.[29] Labor productivity growth is on very different paths in developing countries, with healthy levels in India mostly based in services and even increases in Sub-Saharan Africa, but from very low levels. While there is no single explanation for each country, the ILO suggests one key explanation is lower labor market turnover, with not enough workers moving fast enough from lower to higher productivity jobs.[30] This is an area where better job search and placement systems can aid better labor reallocation, although only at the margins.

All of the policies needed to improve good job creation in developing countries are the subject of much research, writing and debate far outside of the scope of this modest book. This book offers just some pointers to how developing countries can and have adapted services to advance employment connections where jobs are growing or where job change is needed (see Chaps. 4 and 5).

RETHINKING JOB SEARCH INTERMEDIATION WITH A JOBS PROBLEM

Today's developing economies have assuredly *both* an intermediation and a labor supply-demand problem – can't connect the right workers with the right jobs, workers don't have the skills for the jobs available – *along with* a good jobs deficit. In developing countries, one has to think differently about how to make job connections happen when there is both less good employment and less open listing of jobs. Making the job search market work better is one fundamental step, but fixing the jobs deficit will require a larger set of policies working together. This book focuses on one labor policy tool but shows in later chapters how developing countries can adapt this tool to play a supporting role in the larger jobs problem. Chapter 2 starts off by explaining this labor policy tool – what are employment services and how do they fit into the framework of labor and social policies that affect employment. Chapter 3 begins the how-to. It shows Stage 1, how developing countries can create and have created core employment services adapted to less-than-ideal employment conditions. Chapter 4 lays out Stage 2, how developing countries have expanded these core employment services into much more adapted labor intermediation services, drawing in migration support and links to skills training among many ways to adapt to developing country economies. Chapter 5 will return us to the bigger "jobs" and economic growth picture, laying out different ways that these labor intermediation services can and do play a role in education, economic development and social policy advances.

This book thus argues – and this is its more unusual argument – that by getting job search to be more transparent and less about "who you know" in the developing world, developing countries can build "labor intermediation services" that have the ability to link poor job seekers with a more tailored combination of training, social assistance, even economic development efforts directly linked to an actual job. But first let's start to explain more fully what this labor policy tool can and can't do.

NOTES

1. *World Development Report: Jobs: 2013*, World Bank, 2013.
2. Diego F. Angel-Udinola et al., "Public Employment Agencies in the Middle East and North Africa Region," p. 42. The authors note the Egyptian figures are particularly misleading because of the disproportionate use of the public employment service for public sector employment.
3. Stephanie McCrummen, "A Nigerian Neighborhood Symbolizes Nation's Tumble Toward Crisis," *Washington Post*, March 3, 2015.
4. Gustavo Adolfo Garcia and Catia Nicodermo, "Job Search, Wage Inequality, and Neighborhood Channels in Developing Countries," April 2013.
5. *Ibid.*, p. 11.
6. Gustavo Marquez and Cristobal Ruiz-Tagle, *Search Methods and Outcomes in Developing Countries*, 2004.
7. *Ibid.*
8. Paul Gregg, "How Effective Are State Employment Agencies?" 1996.
9. Dante Contreras, et al. "The Role of Social Networks in Employment," July 2007.
10. *Ibid.*
11. "Unemployment as a % of total labor force, 2012" World Bank Jobs Databank, http://datatopics.worldbank.org/jobs/topic/employment.
12. "Youth Unemployment: 2013", World Bank Jobs Databank, http://data.worldbank.org/indicator/SL.UEM.1524.ZS/countries/1W-4E-ZF-XQ-S3?display=graph
13. Gary Fields, *Working Hard, Working Poor*, 2013.
14. *World Employment and Social Outlook: 2015*, International Labour Organization, p. 28.
15. *Workforce Connections: Kenya Youth Assessment*, U.S. Agency for International Development, August 2014, p. vi.
16. *Ibid.*, p. 28.

17. *Global Employment Trends for Youth: 2015,* 2015.
18. *Ibid.*
19. World Bank, *Migration and Remittances Factbook 2011*, p. 4–5.
20. The focus of such services is on economic migrants; the flows of refugees, particularly from the most recent crisis in Syria, represent a more complex international problem outside the scope of this book.
21. Manpower Group, *2015 Talent Shortage Survey*, 2015, p. 6.
22. Countries are grouped in income classifications from World Bank fiscal year 2016 data, http://data.worldbank.org/about/country-and-lending-groups#Low_income
23. Manpower Group, *2015 Talent Shortage Survey*, 2015, Appendix.
24. *Skills for the 21st Century: Indonesia Assessment*, p. 18.
25. *World Employment and Social Outlook: 2015*, p. 28.
26. *Ibid.*
27. "Countries Where Poverty Rates Increased by Heads of Households" International Labour Organization,http://www.ilo.org/global/about-the-ilo/multimedia/maps-and-charts/WCMS_369630/lang–en/index.htm.
28. *World Employment and Social Outlook: 2015*, 2015, p. 16.
29. *The Productivity Brief: 2015*, The Conference Board, 2016.
30. *Ibid.*, p. 25.

CHAPTER 2

Employment and Labor Intermediation Services: What Are They and What Are They Good For?

Employment services are designed to match job seekers – whether unemployed or in a job – with available jobs. If done well, they fulfill three key labor market objectives: (1) reducing the time it takes to find a job (good for both the worker and the employer); (2) increasing the percentage of workers obtaining a job; and (3) enabling a better fit between the worker (their skills) and the job they are doing. A better fit of worker-to-job has related labor market benefits as well – the worker can be more productive, stay longer at the job (e.g. reduced job rotation and job volatility), and hopefully gain a higher wage due to the better, more productive fit. Employment services were never intended to be needed by everyone looking for a job, but as laid out in the previous chapter, it is clear that many disadvantaged workers in developing countries don't have efficient or effective methods, particularly formal ones, to get jobs. Having in mind these gains of speed, placement and increased quality, we can both begin to see where employment services may fit in the set of needed policies for developing countries regarding employment *and* why adapting such services to local labor markets may assist in rectifying a range of employment and skill disconnections.

Both public and privately-run employment services to help job seekers get jobs have had more than a century of practice in the industrialized countries. Even so, no single model has emerged; they are still changing and adapting operating models to changing economies and technology. The basic services and economic rationale of what is known as the active labor market policy of employment services, however, are fundamentally similar,

© The Author(s) 2017

J. Mazza, *Labor Intermediation Services in Developing Economies*,

DOI 10.1057/978-1-137-48668-4_2

even if ever modernizing to newer forms. "Active" in this sense means actively matching a worker to a job or inserting a worker into employment.

This chapter discusses in detail the basics of employment services – the core functions, record and rationales – and then describes the more advanced version of labor intermediation services which is triggered when an employment service moves forward to create a set of extended services adapted to very different labor markets and national policies. From the basics of employment/intermediation services – what they are and who delivers them – the chapter then goes on to discuss what they are good for (and not good for!) in the broader framework of other labor market and social policies.

EMPLOYMENT SERVICES: THEIR RECORD, AND THEIR ECONOMIC AND SOCIAL RATIONALES

Employment services have been identified by a wide range of impact evaluations as the most cost-effective active labor market policy.[1] That is, for not so much money (relative to, say, training), employment services offer a comparatively good investment in terms of impacts on getting a job, and sometimes getting a better paying job. The principal impact found is on increased employment rates over those who did not receive the service. Only some services were found to improve earnings, that is are able to help job seekers find a job at a higher wage than they had before.[2] Improving the quality of the job acquired, measured by a higher income, is a particular area in which better designed and better performing services can improve impacts. Studies on the United Kingdom's performance-based systems (Employment Zones and the New Deal) found they worked best for those with a better employment record and were less effective for those without qualifications, had been unemployed for longer and had an unstable pattern of employment.[3]

While impact evaluations for employment services in developing countries are much fewer than those for developed countries, Gordon Betcherman and colleagues at the World Bank have found developing country evaluation results consistent with those of developed countries.[4] One of the few impact evaluations of a developing country employment service was in Mexico City; this evaluation interestingly found positive impacts for men but not for women.[5] This points to the value of tailoring service design to developing country labor markets which may have more inherent discrimination. Mexico, for example, has high levels of occupational segregation for women, even compared to other middle-income developing economies. This may mean making job placement more effective for women may require greater efforts to not reinforce existing occupational segregation by placing women disproportionately in the same low-wage jobs considered only women's work. Overall, employment services have been found to be more effective when the economy is growing. This is hardly rocket science – more job placement can happen when there are more jobs being generated. Without extensive job openings, employment services can only have an impact at the margin for some workers (e.g. via information and cost/time savings and aiding more efficient job rotation), but they may have more limited impact in volume terms during poor economic times.

Whether by public, private or non-profit providers, investing to expand employment and later labor intermediation services in developing countries can be motivated by both economic and social rationales. If developing economies generated employment easily, if only those who wanted to be unemployed or part-time employed were so, and if workers could easily find good paying work, there would be no need for labor intermediation services. In that case, we could end this book at page one!

But labor markets do not operate perfectly in any country of the world. Their imperfections are more severe and have greater consequences in countries with high rates of poverty, discrimination and social tension. What are those economic and social factors that impede the ability of workers to find good jobs, assuming some exist? Reviewing these economic and social rationales for supporting more and better labor intermediation services helps both in understanding what problems labor intermediation services may be able to address and why such services may have different emphases, targets and program linkages in the very different labor markets in the developing world. What are some of these problems that more intensified job search assistance could help address but not fix completely?

- **Information barriers.** Both workers and firms, particularly in developing countries, face limited (at best) information. For workers, it is important to know by whom and where jobs are being offered, and what skills are needed, so they can plan education, training and job search around getting a job in their home country. For firms, the information required includes knowing where to find the workers for available jobs; knowing/anticipating their own skill and workforce needs in the near future (e.g. what they should be planning for); and knowing where to locate their business to get the best access to qualified labor. Perfectly clearing labor markets (where labor supply fits perfectly with labor demand) assume that workers and firms all have perfect information. Labor intermediation services cannot deliver this labor market *perfection*, but labor market information systems and job banks can reduce informational deficits for a segment of the labor market that can be matched through better information.

- **Costs/time of job search/finding employees.** Without perfect information, both job seekers and employers incur "search costs" – time and money in finding the right job or the right employee. While research shows that job search is improved when using multiple methods, evaluations of employment services show that they reduce both the time and the costs of making a job match.[6] Costs include lost time, lost money, and lower productivity (which costs time and money) if a less productive person is in the job or the firm produces less for greater unit cost. These productivity costs are not just for the individual or firm, but added together affect national productivity. Search costs also rise because of "coordination frictions": the right person applies for the job just after it is filled or the right person takes another job causing the search to begin all over again.

- **Labor isn't one size.** Perfectly operating labor markets also don't happen because labor is not standardized and people are not perfectly replaceable or interchangeable. Employers may need to interview to find the right person and they may have not clearly articulated the skills they need. Labor intermediation services are an indirect way of improving the specifications of a job, and helping make more efficient internal (firm) human resource processes.[7]

- **Un- and Underemployment inefficiencies (national and individual).** Involuntary unemployment, under and sub-employment all have economic, social and human capital costs, both to economies and to the individuals and families facing them.

- **Productivity and income losses due to job volatility.** Not having the right person in the right job at the right wage is one of a number of factors behind job change. While the rate of job and career changes has been increasing for today's more skills-based modern economies, frequent job loss and change for poor workers in developing economies can also be a sign of vulnerability and excessive productivity loss. While statistics on job rotation rates in developing economies is highly limited, some job change leads to costly losses in productivity and income. This has been seen in developing economies: wages so low that workers move to other jobs for the most minimal increase in pay; workers fired to save a day of pay, in a daily and endless cycle of hiring and firing in a low productivity business model.

- **Skills mismatches.** Not enough workers skilled in the jobs demanded are a feature of developing and developed countries alike, as presented in Chapter 1. Labor intermediation services are not the principal policy to address this problem, but they can play a short-term role in addressing mismatches due to location and poor information (job seekers and the jobs not in the same town/city) and play a medium-term information role in helping articulate where labor demand is going.
- **Labor market discrimination.** Job seekers may never get considered or accepted for employment due to their race, ethnicity, gender, caste or poverty – pure labor market discrimination. While there are many factors behind this discrimination, labor intermediation services have a more pressing social and economic rationale in developing economies with decades – no, centuries – of discrimination. Such services may themselves be sources of discrimination if they are known to be largely only working with, say, educated males (e.g. a concern raised in Lebanon). How to effectively combat such discrimination through more open and fairer hiring practices and services is more complex and merits further attention and study.
- **Involuntary informality.** Labor intermediation services have largely been an instrument for formal sector jobs. Informal jobs, those under the legal radar defined as jobs without benefits, can comprise from 50% (Brazil) to 90+ % (India) of employment. Lowering informality would never be a direct rationale for investing in labor intermediation services; more evidence from different developing economies is needed to see if formal methods can be an instrument *at the margin* for moving workers who are involuntarily in informal jobs into formal jobs that they might not have access to. As mentioned in Chapter 1, there is some evidence that only informal search in developing countries increases the probability of finding only an informal sector job.[8] Labor intermediation services, cannot affect the broader factors creating informality in an economy. What is least known, though, is whether intermediation services could play a complementary role in supporting formal employment in developing countries by increasing the tools for formal job searches and providing greater transparency in formal job openings. While intermediation and formal job search cannot "create" formal employment, it may possibly have a role in improving the odds of finding formal sector work.
- **Jobs as more than jobs.** It is appropriate to end this review of social and economic rationales for investment in employment/labor

intermediation services with stating the obvious. Moving people into better jobs, even if the numbers are not very large at first, has other social and longer-term impacts on individuals, families and communities. Social rationales include the acquisition of social and work habits, self-esteem through work, reduced criminality and addiction, and greater confidence and support for institutions.

From an understanding of the record and economic and social rationales for employment services, to a closer look at what they consist of.

Employment Services: The Core Services

There is a "core" set of services needed to make job placement happen. If you don't get core services to any volume or quality, it doesn't much matter how many other services you add. Core employment services are those services needed to provide basic job matching/placement functions: an active list of job vacancies; a register of job seekers; and methods for making the match – either via job counselors at walk-in centers, or by stimulating independent search via computer listings, announcements of job openings, and job fairs. The three core services can be more clearly defined as:

- **A job "bank":** A listing of available positions together with a listing of available job seekers. More and more this is computerized and sophisticated so that searches and referrals can be based on skill requirements and experience needed. Just as common in low-income countries, however, are random pieces of paper and flyers on the wall!
- **Job search assistance and counseling:** Humans assisting job seekers through the process of identifying what type of job they might seek, what types of jobs are out there, and how to think about sequencing jobs into a career (more advanced) to accompany the use of a job bank. With advances in technology there is a tendency to think this process can be automated to the maximum degree, with online résumé preparation, online job-matching sites, and direct contacts with listed employers via the telephone or internet. In labor markets with a lot of transparency, and particularly for better educated job seekers, a lot can indeed be automated but this often needs to be created and kept relevant by skilled humans. With varying levels of automation, this core service is actually a diverse set of services with the same purpose but with locally adapted forms: counselors at a

walk-in center; courses/workshops to teach job search and interview techniques in a local context, given at a walk-in center, community center, or via a mobile van (e.g. in Jalisco, Mexico). For much low-skilled work where a CV (*curriculum vitae*) is not common practice, job search assistance may mean something as simple as being an inter-mediary (e.g. writing a letter, making a phone call) to an employer who would never open their door to a stranger (see Chap. 3).

- **Job placement:** The core function/service that results from having the above two core services working well is placement in a job. As multiple job search methods are generally needed to get a job, it is challenging, but essential, for job placement to be measured and reported. A good placement means both that the person stays in the job (often measured in 3–12-month intervals) and receives a wage that enables them to stay.

"Core" does not mean easy or simple. Core employment services require continual work with local employers to maintain a large and active enough list of openings and skilled workers and good management systems capable of placing or referring workers to new jobs, as well as the provision of relevant labor market and career guidance. Remember the services work at the margin between a worker and a job, seeking to reduce the time a worker is unemployed and the time a firm goes without the workers it needs. Regaining – or gaining – the trust of employers in the developing world to enable placement via "intermediating" between employer and potential employee is the greatest challenge in creating any viable core service. Chapter 3 will review how a private sector strategy has become *the* critical element for developing countries even to develop the most basic service. Without it, they can get a long list of job seekers with no jobs to match them to.

Table 2.1 summarizes the "core" services provided by all public or pri-vate employment services with their target clients. Most employment ser-vices have added more services, called here extended services, as they have joined with other social or economic services under the same roof. Once the range of services goes beyond core employment services, it is more accurate to call them labor intermediation services since they have moved on from the original focus on basic job-matching. They are called extended services here because they "extend" the core functions into deeper employ-ment connections and human capital development. Importantly, core ser-vices must be in place and working well for any extended services to have success in aiding better placement and employment.

Table 2.1 Service types – core functions versus extended services

	Service type	*Client*
Core functions	Job search assistance/counseling Job placement	Job seekers and employers
	Job bank (vacancies and job seekers)	Job seekers and employers
Extended services intermediation "Plus"	Management of training or other active labor market policies	Employers; workers; job seekers
	Migrant support services	Internal & external migrants; employers
	Microenterprise/self-employment support	Self-employed
	Placement services for employers	Employers
Support services	Labor market information systems	Job seekers, employers, educational institutions
	Specialized human resources services to employers	Employers
	Social service gateway/unemployment insurance administration	Workers; job seekers; unemployed

Who Provides These Services?

Before delving into the extended services, a quick look at who provides these services whether core or extended. The active labor market policy to improve the match of job seeker to job has long been associated with just one delivery agent – a publically-financed public employment service (PES). This means public funds finance the offices, the counselors, the online and walk-in services. But the truth is that the same function has from the outset also been done *simultaneously* by a set of public, private and non-profit institutions, albeit these very different agents usually serve different clientele according to different financing models.

Many countries used to follow a International Labour Organization (ILO) convention (since repealed) which prohibited private employment services from operating or charging a job seeker a fee (employers generally can be charged fees). It has taken years for many developed and developing countries to formally remove this restriction, even while it was often ignored. It is one of many factors – more important are demand and market size – to explain why there are far fewer private providers doing this work in developing countries. In Tunisia, for example, private providers of placement services are still prohibited by law.

Moving to today's understanding of who provides employment services: public employment agencies, private employment or recruitment agencies, such as Manpower Inc., and non-profit agencies all conduct the three core services. Internet-only websites such as Monster.com or Caribbeanjobs.com are tools of job search and not of employment or labor intermediation services unless they provide all the core functions. In the developing and developed world, local services are also increasingly run by non-profit organizations or community organizations, such as Catholic churches in Lima, Peru, who have helped members of their congregations find work with local parishioners, or NGOs which can integrate job placement as part of the delivery of another service (an intermediation "plus" service). It should be noted, though, that when impact evaluations are done on the active labor market policy tool of employment services, they typically only measure the impact of the public service, even if the public service supports or its information and other services help the private and non-profit sectors to also have an intermediation impact.

Financing, coverage, and success rates can vary markedly *between* different public, private and non-profit actors. Public expenditure for public employment services in developing countries is and always will be constrained by limited public funds. That's why public-private-non-profit partnerships become more essential to public employment services in developing countries than they have been in the developed countries (and even in the developed countries they are playing more roles). Public employment services in Africa working alone are noted as being particularly limited. When they do exist, their coverage is limited and there is not enough financing to extend to the rural areas or to have many local offices. A recent review found African public employment services lacked key mechanisms to serve clients and had "limited capacity" to respond to client needs, particularly of the most vulnerable.[9] Private and non-profit services are financed either using a business model (e.g. firms pay for placement services, such as Manpower Inc. or private migration agencies are paid to process and send migrants to high-income Middle East nations) or by a foreign or domestic donations model that combines grants with perhaps some money selling their services (e.g. partial self-financing). Private employment agencies are traditionally found to concentrate on either of two markets: the "higher end" of the labor market – high tech and professional workers or large cohorts of low-skilled workers (e.g. administrative staff, construction for work abroad). Non-profit organizations, working with donations, are more able to concentrate directly on the poor and groups that face labor market discrimination and barriers to employment, such as women, youth, indigenous populations, and Afro descendants in non-African and Afro-descendent majority countries.

EXTENDED SERVICES: GROWING INTO LABOR INTERMEDIATION SERVICES

Why do most employment services – public, private or non-profit – move quickly into, or even start out with, more than just the core functions? The simplest explanation is that job placement rarely works as simply as a Match.com single moment – job seeker A with good CV and advice matched with perfect job opening B equals an employment marriage (many find that Match.com doesn't work that way either!). The extended services can serve *either* as incentives for creating placement openings where they might not otherwise appear, called "intermediation plus" type extended services in this book, *or* they provide information or support services that get job seekers in the door. Table 2.1 lists the three types of extended services discussed in this book: intermediation plus, information, and support services.

Particularly in employment-poor developing countries, where employers either through culture, custom, or bad experience will not list a job, where the economy isn't generating jobs or the applicants don't have the basic skills for the available jobs (large skill mismatches), offering only the traditional core functions would likely limit the reach of the service. The challenge for developing countries is both institutional and strategic – being highly selective in identifying one or two extended services to start off with. Starting selective is important so as to build institutional capacity and use the extended service to build credibility with the private sector and use the extended service to help improve the performance of the core functions. These extended services may or may not be run by the same institution that does the core job-matching functions, but connecting these efforts is very important in getting labor markets moving in developing countries. How developing countries can use extended services to build core functions and improve overall performance is discussed at length in Chapter 4. Here is a quick explanation of extended services in the three categories used in this book. These services come into play selectively in the later evolution of a public, private or non-profit intermediation service. For a more extensive review of these and more extended services, the reader can fast forward to Stage 2 in Chapter 4. It is worth repeating here that employment services of all origins principally focus on formal, wage and salaried work. It is through extended services that some adaptations can be made to other forms of work, although their comparative advantage does lie in supporting formal employment.

"Intermediation Plus" Extended Services

Extended services may be grouped into three types. The first I am calling "intermediation plus" to highlight that they seek to ultimately place a person in a job but that they do so by helping to overcome some obstacles that cannot be fixed via simple job matching (the cheapest, easiest and fastest route to a job if matching is all that is needed). A key feature is the use of the service, or the incentive provided by the service, to help pry open a hidden job market. *Training or wage subsidy programs* are the most common form of extended service. I have seen this work throughout the developing world – when an employer who doesn't think they have a job or is unwilling to offer a job to a stranger. They may be convinced to supervise a "free" trainee or accept a cash wage subsidy and, afterwards, may hire the person. The more effective of these "training for job placement" programs require a percentage of the trainees (typically 50–60%) to be hired. Training programs have various lengths, content and track records – not all types do or are intended to lead to job placement. They can be applied to those looking for a job, or can be for "active" workers currently employed. To be considered "intermediation plus," we're talking only about training used for outsiders to help them get into the labor market. Training with the best record is "on the job" – that is, on a work site, using the equipment and methods of an actual workplace. The training or wage subsidy service referred to here can either be an actual program managed by the same people who manage core job placement or can be a referral service, in which job seekers are sent to or are provided listings of local training programs. Both training and wage subsidies are tools of "active" labor market policies and have different functions than job placement, discussed more at the end of this chapter.

A second "intermediation plus" service found principally in developing countries is *migrant support services*. Most migrants from the South migrate for work without any support or service and this has fed a much larger international crisis as the daily headlines from Syria, Libya, and Bangladesh (among the many) attest. Authorized migration from a home country to a foreign job, however, can be aided, made safer, and even circular, with greater oversight being exercised to guard against exploitation. For external migrants, particularly in seasonal agricultural and tourism work, services can screen workers, insure their fair payment and even supervise their return. A range of country examples under four types of migrant services linked to labor intermediation as well as a third extended service – microenterprise or self-employment programs – are discussed in greater detail in Chapter 4.

A final "intermediation plus" service is placement and support work done directly for employers outside of any open public listing. Employers may want private screening done of applicants, and/or interviews set up or even conducted, typically for time and efficiency reasons. They may be too small an employer to do this themselves; they may not want to use their scarce personnel for tasks that people skilled in human resources could handle more efficiently. This can be a service introduced very early in order to build confidence with private employers – e.g. they might list jobs in the future if this works – as well as enable a service to develop a market in specific types of employment (e.g. high tech) that needs specialized screening. The fee-based service could include screening, interviewing and testing potential candidates for employment. These services can thus serve multiple functions of increasing job placements, getting more vacancy listings (thereby strengthening core services over time), and bringing in revenue for cash-starved public employment services.

Information and Program Administration Services

The second and third types of services *complement* and *support* the core mission of job placement of an employment service, now an emerging labor intermediation service. They are not, though, an indirect way to expand job listings or placements as we can argue that "intermediation plus" services do.

Information services provide data and information on trends related to choosing or advancing in jobs. The most central and first established information system is a labor market information system or labor market "observatory." It is hard to provide good job counseling if you don't know where the local economy is going, or hard to recommend to a job seeker they undergo training if you don't have the information base on where employment is growing and which institutions' graduates get jobs. A labor market information system requires a level of systematic labor market information (e.g. annual, quarterly labor market surveys) as well as an institutional investment to keep it continually relevant. The evolution and use of labor market information systems is a featured element in the second stage of labor intermediation services (Chap. 4).

Program Administration-Coordination. Labor intermediation services in their more advanced stages also administer or have on site in their offices a host of other social, labor, and economic services. In most of the advanced countries some form of employment service began together with an unemployment insurance (UI) program. The link was explicit in some European countries – the unemployed needed to walk into a public employment service and demonstrate they were looking for work to pick up their checks. Only an employment service would have the records and the capability to document a UI recipient's efforts at job search. In Switzerland, a UI recipient must see an employment counselor at the local PES and receive job referrals or demonstrate specifically which firms he/she has solicited a job from. Administration or links with unemployment insurance or other social-economic programs is still a core function of most developed countries' public employment services, even if some, like the United States, have long ago lost an effective job search requirement for UI. Unemployment insurance is a rare luxury in the low-income developing world, although more systems are found in middle-income developing countries, including in Eastern Europe, North Africa, Turkey, the Southern Cone of Latin America, and the Caribbean. The fundamental consideration for developing countries in utilizing public employment services for UI administration or coordination via enforcement of a work search requirement or verification of residency (e.g. that the UI recipient hasn't migrated out of the country) is one of sequencing and labor market realities. If core employment services are not yet developed enough to serve the incoming unemployed, then requiring additional bureaucratic hoops to be jumped through to prove work search cripples both the PES, and the motivation/time of the UI recipient.

Beyond unemployment insurance, more and more countries – including many developing countries – are moving towards consolidating a number of social/economic services in the same center or location as the labor intermediation service. Typically these are government services or non-profit-run services; social services such as income support to the poor or aid to single mothers; and, of particular relevance to developing countries, business services such as the range of services to register, start, and support a small business. Developing countries which have pioneered social assistance in the form of conditional and non-conditional cash transfers are also now pioneering new forms of integrating or linking social assistance and employment support, as discussed in the final chapter. The principles are similar to those of other administration or co-location programs, to link incentives between social assistance and exiting social assistance to employment, or to aid a range of non-employment barriers to work. This new thinking is creating even wider forms of intermediation services which represent a brighter future for the developing world (Chap. 5).

WHAT THEY CAN AND CANNOT DO: AN ACTIVE LABOR MARKET AND SOCIAL POLICY REALITY CHECK

Labor intermediation/employment services are considered one of a set of "active" labor market policies a country can employ. Their principal objective is to increase employment or income or productivity on the job. "Passive" labor market policies are essentially income supports when a person is outside of employment, with unemployment insurance as the principal policy. Early retirement and severance payments are also passive labor market policies. Protecting incomes is important, as it enables someone to look for a better job, maintains family incomes, and keeps communities viable in crisis times.

Labor intermediation services, or what used to be called employment services, comprise one of three principal active labor market policy instruments. They began in some European countries after WWI, but active labor market policies in the developed countries really took off in the 1960s. As we have amply explained, their purpose is to enable job seekers to find a job faster and more quickly than they would without any formal policy or services. One can see that their principal impact is short-term – shortening the time of unemployment or between jobs, improving the match with the next job.

Training – the second and most well-known active labor market policy – has a different purpose. It is supposed to help improve the skills of workers, some for basic job skills, and some being highly technical that takes a long time. It can be of very varied duration and cost, with the most effective forms conducted in the workplace. Apprenticeship is a form of longer-term training getting a lot of popular press, but its best results are in business cultures with traditions of such investments, such as Germany and Austria. Training has been found to have little impact in the short term, but better results in the medium term.[10] It is far more expensive per individual than employment/labor intermediation services, so key aspects to keep in mind are that it matters how effective the training is, whether it is training for a real job, and whether the benefits justify the costs. Given these key differences in costs and impacts, the diagnosis given to an individual job seeker's employment profile by a labor intermediation service is critical. If they have the skill set for immediate job placement that should be the primary intervention, with the labor intermediation service possibly helping to guide medium-term training and career development. But clearly, for other individuals not job-ready, referral to training, back to education or another instrument is more appropriate. The distinct active labor market policies should be understood to work better for distinct types of labor market problems (see Table 2.2).

A third active labor market policy is wage subsidies. These are essentially partial subsidies to induce employers to take on a certain worker who will hopefully be hired at the end of the period. Wage subsidies are often used to give short-term incentives for hiring disadvantaged workers (e.g. persons with disabilities), incentives during economic downturns when firms are not hiring and unemployment is high, or incentives to locate or hire workers in poor areas.[11] Wage subsidies can be effective if used very judiciously, but they are expensive to employ if the job seeker could get a job without their wage being subsidized. Wage subsidies have also been modified to cover on-the-job training periods – the initial months when a worker is being trained on the job before they are fully productive.

Two other types of policies have been considered, at times, in the active labor market policy basket: temporary employment programs and small business development. Temporary employment programs have a record in both Latin America and East Asia, albeit not a particularly successful one, as a post-crisis labor market policy. These are temporary jobs (typically of two to six months), either paid (by the government) employment in a private firm or in a community job (e.g. street cleaning). While these policies are helpful to diffuse a local employment crisis, as in Haiti after the 2010 earthquake or Indonesia in financial crisis, they do not have a good record of being valued in the labor market after the temporary job ends. Such policies play a more important social and political role quite distinct

Table 2.2 Tailoring active labor market programs to labor market needs

Labor market needs or problem	Program types	Special targeting
Moderate cyclical downturns	Direct job creation (e.g., public works) Wage subsidies Training (subsidies or grants to workers or employers) Self-employment support	Vulnerable groups (with least resiliency) Hard-hit regions and industries
Reduce structural imbalances	Employment services (e.g. information, search assistance, relocation assistance) Training Wage subsidies	Proximate regions, industries, or occupations
Improve general labor market functioning	Employment services Training (e.g. apprenticeship, school-to-work transition)	All
Enhance skills and productivity	Training and retraining (including in-firm, apprenticeship)	At risk or disadvantaged worker categories (especially for retraining)
Support disadvantaged or at-risk workers	Employment services (counseling, job search assistance) Training (e.g. grants, subsidies) Wage subsidies	At-risk or disadvantaged worker categories

Source: Adapted from Gordon Betcherman et al., *Active Labor Market Programs: Policy Issues for East Asia*, 2000.

from the labor market speed/better efficiency role of labor intermediation services.

A quick summary of the appropriate uses of labor intermediation services versus other types of labor market policies is provided in Table 2.2. This is based on impact evaluations and other evidence. It is very important to see such services as better adapted for only certain types of employment needs and to look at their ability to refer workers to a more effective intervention for other labor market needs. There are many barriers to employment in the developing world. Applying the right instrument(s) to the right problem at a sustainable cost requires constant tinkering and rethinking, adjusting to changing local employment conditions.

By improving the speed and quality of job matches, intermediation services are best designed (Table 2.2) for reducing structural imbalances (by shortening unemployment spells, reducing underemployment, reducing job turnover) and improving general market functioning (via better information, less discriminatory hiring, on-the-job productivity). Since they do not change the educational or job qualifications of a worker, employment or intermediation services would not be particularly effective in delivering new skills for workers not ready for employment (although they can screen and refer job seekers). Nor can they overcome more entrenched social barriers to job entry, such as alcoholism or child care responsibilities. However, they can serve to better identify and screen for these barriers so that the job seeker may ultimately be employed. Here we see the complementary role of training as well as social policy interventions to address the specific employment barriers faced by workers.

Employment/labor intermediation services cannot place workers into non-existent jobs or create employment. They may, however, have distinct roles in times of high unemployment as a platform for other active labor market policies. Ironically, it is often an employment crisis which has fueled national investment in employment services, such as in Korea and Mexico, which were able to rebalance service delivery in better employment times.

Active and passive labor market policies should not be viewed as two isolated camps; the best types are highly complementary. We discussed earlier how labor intermediation services can work with unemployment insurance; in fact, most OECD (Organization of Economic Cooperation and Development) countries require some form of linkage between these two types of policies as there is an increasing concern about getting the long-term unemployed "activated" into the labor market. In most OECD nations, passive and active measures have been developed simultaneously, if not passive measures first. Passive measures, by and large, are more costly and, in recent decades, most OECD nations have moved to emphasize active over passive measures. Of the 24 OECD countries submitting spending data, only 5 – Denmark, the Czech Republic, Hungary, Norway and Sweden – spent more on active measures.[12] Developing countries, if one is to generalize, have invested first in active labor market policies, often training and vocational education systems, where poor quality and lack of connection to private sector demand is more the rule than the exception. Passive policies, largely unemployment insurance systems, are far more recent, but are generally more limited in coverage in the developing world, with important exceptions in Eastern Europe and middle-income countries, such as Chile and the Caribbean. One can argue that severance payments have been legally mandated in many developing countries, but these apply only to formal work and are paid by the employing firm with no government financing or insurance. Severance payments have such a spotty record of being paid in developing countries that they do not serve as an income support policy, particularly for the lower end of the labor force. In relation to labor market intermediation services, passive income supports, whether unemployment insurance or cash transfer assistance, should be looked at for their tighter connection to more effective job search. This is especially true for developing countries where drawing on scarce fiscal resources and using worker-firm contributory schemes have great trade-offs. Any passive program, however modest, should learn from the mistakes of many OECD nations which felt UI had become too generous and less of a mechanism to facilitate good re-entry into the labor market.

The direct effect of all active labor market policies on employment, unemployment and earnings has been summarized by Calmfours as threefold, the first aspect of which is directly related to employment services: (1) improved job matching; (2) increased and enhanced labor supply; and, (3) increased labor demand.[13] Any deadweight effects, those going to individuals who would have succeeded to the same extent without the intervention, lower the cost-benefit of active labor market policies.

It is also important to remember that employment services and their more advanced cousin, labor intermediation services, operate within given national policy contexts, business environments and labor regulations (e.g. on hiring and firing). Active labor market policies can complement but cannot overcome particularly restrictive regulations on hiring, firing and benefit levels. One of the few studies to have reviewed both labor policy and employment service effectiveness found, on labor policies, a negative correlation only on one type of labor regulation – the strictness of dismissal protection legislation. This study found the impact was on employment probability, that is, firms being less willing to hire formally if it is very difficult to dismiss the worker.[14] Suffice to say, among the limitations to getting formal jobs openly listed is a regulatory environment that heavily disadvantages new hires. Similarly, high labor taxes can also discourage employment as in the countries of Eastern Europe and Central Asia, notably Montenegro, Macedonia and Serbia.[15] In short, except for the narrow area of dismissal legislation and even here this correlation was not strongly negative, employment services were found to have positive impacts despite very different labor policy contexts.

Some final evidence on active labor market policies. The overwhelming majority of impact evaluations on active labor market policies that examine employment services measure the impact at the individual level: higher numbers of individuals getting jobs faster using services than without them. As in overall labor market analysis, less is known about the macro or general equilibrium effects in terms of reducing national unemployment or underemployment. Dan Finn, summarizing OECD evidence for the developing countries of Latin America and the Caribbean, found macroeconomic impacts such that employment increased and unemployment fell more quickly in those countries that had redesigned their active labor market policies including public employment services within a comprehensive activation – or job-linkage – strategy.[16] He argues that earlier US and European reforms aimed at "broadening coverage, tightening eligibility, increasing conditionality and making work pay" increased the effectiveness of the emergency measures taken to deal with the shocks of economic crisis. Finally, the international literature, which records consistently positive findings on labor intermediation, seldom argues for the wholesale jettisoning of other active labor market measures in favor of services and sanctions. Rather, they indicate that employment services would be particularly useful in reducing short-term unemployment and in adapting to economic crises working in a complementary fashion with other active labor market policies. They also point out that, while large-scale training and temporary employment were less effective active labor market policies, there was evidence that design features and targeting were key to more positive results for medium-term employment even in these two labor market policies.

Building from Core to Labor Intermediation Services in Stages

Strengthening the link between labor and social policy programs and labor intermediation systems is just one of a number of areas where labor intermediation services are taking on a different character from labor intermediation systems which evolved in the developed economies over decades, and now centuries, with far greater resources.

This book now takes you through rethinking labor intermediation for developing economies in a global age in stages: Stage 1, building core services (Chap. 2); Stage 2, expanding coverage, services and innovation (Chap. 3); Stage 3, linking to social, economic and workforce policies (although still in evolution). These stages are based on "hands-on" experience with basic employment services in developing countries, watching some evolve through Stage 2 and some in the starting gates for Stage 3. Each of these Stages, from 1 to 3, represents a progression and advance of intermediation as an active labor market policy. Each stage has distinct design, operational and performance features as well as very different national, regional and sub-regional variations.

NOTES

1. For a listing of studies see Alessio J.G. Brown and Johannes Koettl, "Active Labor Market Programs – Employment Gain or Fiscal Drain?" 2015.
2. David Card et al., "Active Labor Market Policy Evaluations: A Meta-Analysis," 2010.
3. Dan Finn, *The Welfare Market*, 2009.
4. Gordon Betcherman et al. "Impacts of Active Labor Market Programs," January 2004.
5. Roberto Flores-Lima, "*Una Evaluacion de Impacto del Servicio de Empleo de la Ciudad de Mexico*," 2005.
6. Jochen Kluve, "The Effectiveness of European Active Labor Market Programs," February 2010.
7. An example can be found in Box 5.1.
8. Gustavo Marquez and Cristobal Tagle-Ruiz, *Search Methods and Outcomes in Developing Countries*, 2004.
9. *The World of Public Employment Services*, Inter-American Development Bank, 2015, p. 18.
10. David Card et al., "Active Labor Market Policy Evaluations: A Meta-Analysis," 2010.
11. When the incentive is given as a tax reduction to the firm, and not a tax incentive for hiring a worker, then the incentive is not considered an active labor market policy instrument.
12. Figures from 2013, "Public expenditures of LMP [Labor Market Policies] by Main Categories, % of GDP," http://stats.oecd.org/Index.aspx?DatasetCode=LMPEXP
13. Lars Calmfors, "Active Labour Market Policies and Unemployment: A Framework for Analysis of Crucial Design Features," 1994.
14. David Card et al., "Active Labor Market Policy Evaluations: A Meta-Analysis," 2010.
15. Omar Arias and Carolyn Sanchez-Paramo, *Back-to-Work: Growing with Jobs in Eastern Europe and Central Asia*, p. 72.
16. Dan Finn, *Design and Effectiveness of Active Labor Market Policies in the OECD*, 2011.

CHAPTER 3

Stage 1: Building Core Employment Services

How does one create a service to deliver core employment services in poor developing countries even if the target is first a small number of formal jobs? To start, few developing countries are beginning from zero in Stage 1. It is more common for a developing country to have or have had some form of small, outdated and obscure public employment service (PES), serving few job seekers. Stage 1 countries may also have a few scattered private placement firms, typically in the capital city. These are likely storefront firms operating with little connection to public offices or the larger national labor market. There may also be some strong non-governmental organizations (NGOs) supporting job placement as part of a community-based program. While this existing infrastructure may be taken into account, relaunching core employment services in today's developing economies requires something wholly different to start – a strategy and defined partnership with the private sector.

This chapter examines how to build, rebuild or re-establish a more modern form of core employment services, termed Stage 1 in this book. These countries are largely lower-income developing countries, such as Guyana, but may include more middle-income countries such as Kenya and the countries of North Africa with a weak private and public institutional base. Most middle-income and transition countries should be considered institutionally at a second stage of services development (Chap. 4).

This chapter lays out key features and strategies of Stage 1 based on the experience of developing countries which have successfully restarted

© The Author(s) 2017   39
J. Mazza, *Labor Intermediation Services in Developing Economies*,
DOI 10.1057/978-1-137-48668-4_3

core employment services and are now well into the later stages of labor intermediation services. It also draws on lessons of the advanced OECD countries that, when appropriately modified, can apply to some developing country markets.

The central starting point for Stage 1 is a jobs strategy for working with the private sector. Three different types of jobs strategies used by developing countries are examined here. As you will soon read, from this strategy follows the rest: how and where core services are best delivered, including choices about the use of storefront locations, online services or whether to locate services within business associations themselves. The chapter also reviews key operational considerations and some service innovations used by developing countries in their early stages. Starting effective, even if small, is key, so performance and monitoring indicators are among the key operational considerations. For countries in Stage 1, while the word "core" sounds simple, getting to a viable volume of jobs and getting employer confidence in a new service requires the combination of a strategy, a viable institutional model, and an innovation or two – or three – taking into account today's electronic economy.

Delivering Core Services in a Global Age

To briefly recap, core services are those needed to make a speedier and better job match. They include some form of job bank that lists and registers available jobs and job seekers in a manner relevant and accessible to both, plus job counseling, and placement or brokerage services to make that match:

- **Job and job seeker register.** Today, this is typically an electronic listing of available jobs and profiles of local job seekers, although in the 1960s all was done on paper. Flyers, newspaper and web-based announcements, and cell phone texts are all instruments designed to promote this common registry. Most developing country services post job announcements in their centers and public places if employers permit. Today, even Stage 1 registers can start out or move quickly to incorporate links to other public or private registries (for example, Manpower Inc., Caribbeanjobs.com) or to download these vacancies into their database.
- **Job search assistance/counseling.** This is typically delivered in three forms: face-to-face meetings with a counselor, workshops on job search and interviews, and online if there's a clientele who will use it. As much as possible, standardizing this assistance into workshops or short modules (a few hours, potentially even online),

permits jobs counselors to use their scarce time to give more personalized attention to the harder-to-serve job seekers.

- **Job brokerage/placement/referral.** This brokerage/job-matching
  function must be part of a core service, though the how varies
  among countries and typically diversifies in approach as a service
  matures. Traditionally, employment service counselors would refer a
  job seeker to a listed job opening. Today, some services just facilitate
  a job match by providing the contact information of the employer
  (although this may not always be the best way to build a service).
  When employers do not want to be overwhelmed with applicants,
  developing country services can also pre-screen applicants from their
  register and send the qualified ones to job vacancies. Over time these
  employers may become ready for public listings.

Simplicity of use and relevance to the local economy in delivering these
core services must be thought through. If it's not easy to use, or there are
not enough staff to help with the initial stages, job seekers and employers
might come once, but not twice, to a service. Advanced services such as
diagnostics of workers and skills as part of the core job search and counseling function are really a Stage 2 advance as they require both experienced
counselors and an evolved local labor market demanding this level of
detail. Find the right adaptation to the local economy and the best delivery
mechanism begins with a strategy for getting private employers to list jobs.

BEGINNING WITH A PRIVATE SECTOR STRATEGY

Whether a country is creating a new institution delivering core services or
reconfiguring an antiquated service that has a poor reputation, step one
is a strategy to start off a service with a viable number of jobs that can
expand realistically from a core base. In short, if you build the service with
jobs, the job seekers will come, but not the other way around. This means
working with a defined group of employers with vacancies to fill or a pressing hiring problem to address, such as high job rotation (tourism and
construction are examples) or attracting workers to isolated locations. A
strategy comes out of engagement and dialogue with employers to understand what types of job placement/rotation problems exist and how they
can best be solved. I have seen many of these dialogues or even just rounds
of visits to employers between the public side (typically the Ministry of
Labor or sometimes a public training institution with an employment legal
mandate) and either the principal employer associations (the best vehicle if

they exist) or major employers, foreign or domestic. The reasons why few jobs are openly competed for has a history which must be recognized in order to start to change it. To gain both employer confidence *and* a ready stream of listings reforming or creating a new service with direct employer participation or links is often the fastest and most sustainable way. To repeat, if you build the service first with jobs, the job seekers will come. The reverse, enlisting job seekers to enroll in a service and then looking for listings, has been tried many times and leads to frustrated job seekers who soon learn not to return.

If I can be explicit here, attempts to lead a dialogue or create a core employment service only from the public sector simply don't work. Often in the highly politicized environment of jobs, governments want to be seen as the ones providing voters with jobs or services, but jobs require employers. The advanced OECD countries did start public employment services without private sector strategies but they had the resources, legal mandates and administration of unemployment insurance all to themselves. The traditional (1950s–60s) model of delivering core services by investing public resources in a solely public employment service – ignoring private and non-profit providers to the extent they exist – simply doesn't and can't happen anymore. Even though the industrialized countries started all-public, they are now all experimenting with different private-public forms.

Developing countries must be more strategic in today's economy. With often small formal sectors and limited transparency in hiring, a developing country's service will not get far by opening its doors and waiting for the voluntary participation of employers. It needs to engage employers as well in order to open jobs along the skills spectrum. Many developing countries' public services have gotten the early reputation of having just low-wage, unskilled labor vacancies. If a service does not seek to build its early reputation on a spectrum of jobs, it will not ultimately serve the poor well, as they will be unable to move out of dead-end unskilled work. True, the more educated and skilled need less job search help. But services can direct the more highly skilled workers to less costly self-serve core services, focusing more person-to-person services on the poor.

By undergoing these initial consultations with employers, it will become clear if available jobs to be listed are too few to start and a different strategy is needed. Developing countries have alternatively led first with short-term skills training leading to job placement, such as the Dominican Republic which initiated first its youth training program and, once a demand base had been built, invested in expanding its employment service.

The strategies to launch a new/rebuilt service in Stage 1 are rarely one. They fall into three broad types, all of which have precedents in developing countries: institutional, sectorial and/or target populations such as youth.

#1 Strategy: Institutional

Creating a new institutional form, be it a network of public, private, NGO centers, a non-profit manager, or shared public-private management, is typically a "game changer" in bringing in employers, achieving better performance, and leaping over past antagonisms. New institutional models are essentially variants of the 100% public financing of 100% public employment offices model, involving private sector organizations and NGOs. They still deliver the core services; the differences come in efficiencies, service delivery, financing and (typically) improved management. In Stage 1, new institutional models enable a developing country to create early employer buy-in (and typically co-financing) and build on institutional capacity and more agile procurement and management than the public sector can offer alone. Institutional models for Stage 1 are used as a key starting point, distinct from the more advanced OECD countries which are using them as a late-stage innovation to improve service and coverage.

Model variety comes in who runs what, in particular who can register and place jobs and job seekers under what umbrella organization. Job listings can be one national register that different types of organizations access or simply a national portal or clearing house. Models include: one national service with both public and non-public (private and/or NGO offices using the same job register, as in Honduras); public and private providers in loose association under a national job register or portal (Mexico in Stage 2); business associations or NGOs running a network of employment centers; or contracting an NGO or firm to run a publically financed service (El Salvador in the 1990s) or contracting an NGO or firm to run a regional office (Ceará, Brazil).

One example among many: Honduras, the poorest country in Latin America and the Caribbean after Haiti, had one of those struggling public employment services (SENANEH, *Servicio Nacional de Empleo de Honduras*) with limited job listings, nearly all unskilled. They did have a network of business associations, many associated with the *maquilla* industry in the North, which regularly hired workers but had problems of high job rotation and needs for skills training. They were initially loath to work with the public sector on a better system. In 2004, before the national employment service was restarted in a new institutional model, there were fewer than 200 private sector companies and even fewer job listings on the public job register. Fewer than 4000 people were served in a country with a national labor force of 2.5 million.[1] A year later, the Ministry of Labor that ran the national employment service signed an agreement to run a public-private service with the Honduran Business Council (*Consejo Hondureño de la Empresa Privada*) with no need for money to change hands. The Ministry of Labor knew employers were not registering their jobs when public employees were taking the information, but employers who regularly attended functions at the offices of the local business council would do so if the person taking the information and doing the placement belonged to the council. So the local business councils set up employment offices in their buildings, providing staff and physical space to take job listings and receive job seekers. The government provided the computers, software, office supplies, and the base electronic platform (shared) called *Empleate*. The government still maintained public sector offices and there was concern at first that, under competition, public employment offices would wither and become irrelevant. Quite the opposite occurred; as Box 3.1 demonstrates, in less than seven years *both* the private offices *and* the public offices dramatically increased their listings and the number of job seekers served. Importantly, the new institutional model provided a more credible way for the national job register to get better employment listings and the model didn't create major bureaucratic obstacles that co-financing or public sector regulations would have imposed.

Box 3.1 Seven Years in Honduras: A Stage 1 Public-Private Launchpad for Jobs

Few people expect much good news in Honduras. It is among the poorer countries in poor Central America. Agricultural work is poorly paid in dire conditions; there is limited formal employment in the *maquilla* textile industries to the North; outmigration to the United States is high. Drug traffickers more and more use Honduras' rural routes to the USA, turning the country into one of the most violent in the world.

In 2004, when the Honduran Public Employment Service started rethinking its basic employment service, relations between the public and private sectors were strained, if not non-existent. Each saw the other as highly politicized. The public sector had a reputation for inefficiency: a bureaucracy without results.

(*continued*)

Box 3.1 (continued)

But the Hondurans engaged the country's major business association, *el Consejo Hondureño de Empresa Privada* (Honduran Private Sector Council or COHEP), in a public-private partnership for employment services that did not require any money to change hands, and the public sector bureaucracy wouldn't be a constraint. The public sector would maintain a national job bank and give computers and training to any COHEP office. The private sector would create a satellite office in their existing facilities with staff to register jobs of their members who regularly came to the offices for meetings. Placement and matching from this now national database could be made either at a public or private sector office.

The change in seven years – throughout and beyond the 2009 financial crisis – is demonstrated below. The public sector had worried that the private sector offices would be competitive with them and that the public sector would lose relevance. In fact, it expanded threefold; the private sector could register jobs with more credibility than the private sector, but the public sector could bring in workers from around the country. By each covering different expenses, the private sector could move forward once the equipment had arrived and decide for itself which offices wanted such a service.

Indicator	2004	2011	% increase
Number of companies registering for jobs	200	10,000	5,000
People served per year	4,000	23,000	575
Number of public offices	2	6	300
Number of networked private sector offices	0	6	600

Source: Jacqueline Mazza, *Fast Tracking Jobs*, 2012

In all cases I have seen, rather than competition between the public and private sectors there has been the opposite – public, private and NGO offices all expanding simultaneously. This is largely because the initial base of open job listings in a developing economy is so small, that there's nowhere to go but up for everyone. Employers are drawn into participating by either direct participation or well-designed outreach incentives to employers. In the case of El Salvador in the late-1990s, an NGO *Fedisal* (*Fundación para la Educación Integral Salvadoreña*) with strong ties to small and medium-sized businesses ran the public service on a contracted-out basis. They were well known to employers in the small and medium-sized business sector and literally went on site to employers to get listings.[2]

To sum up, new institutional models in Stage 1 are derived from a strategy aimed at getting key employers to participate and list jobs. They are both more strategic and less ambitious in scale than the public-private models that can be introduced in Stage 2, discussed in the next chapter, when a country has both a greater public and private institutional base and a wider range of employers who would/could participate. New institutional models can also be employed as part of working with a particular business sector (strategy #2) or working only with a target population, such as youth (strategy #3).

#2 Sector-Based Strategies

In countries where potential formal employment growth is relatively low, sectors are highly concentrated regionally or employment growth depends on attracting new domestic or international investment. A Stage 1 employment service designed to serve all sectors equally in such cases would have little utility for the few business employers who comprise the potential market. A private sector strategy in these cases is to start by focusing on more tailored core services which in later stages can grow into a broader (in terms of sectors) service serving a national market.

In such cases, a private sector strategy focused on the employment needs of the sector(s) could provide the foundation for a new set of core services. These could be delivered by or in partnership with business associations, single large firms with supporting suppliers or sub-contractors, or public offices managed by business oversight-consultation boards, among the many forms. In addition, sectoral strategies may likely bring in an associated sectoral set of vocational-technical schools or school departments that would be a likely source of entry-level workers. I have seen this work in developing countries in the light industry sector, tourism or as a service to support a new foreign investment, such as Korean investment in textile manufacturing in the north of Haiti. Mongolia is seeking to reinvigorate its public employment service by pulling in employers in construction, mining, and the services sectors.

Under a sectoral strategy even in Stage 1, employer needs will typically extend into specialized services to facilitate placement or readiness to work. This can include conducting or linking to training or voc-tech programs, testing of applicants' skill levels, even language training and certification to support call centers. The skills training function might actually predominate, with the intermediation function delivered post-training. Geographic proximity and location are key design features for sector-based strategies, and have included a set of offices on an industrial site and/or offices within relevant training centers. Depending on how specific these services need to be, sector-based core employment services can either be the basis for expanding more broadly into the economy or into other sectors, or may always be a special type of labor intermediation service that retains its special status in a larger system (as in Tunisia, for example) or at some point in the future could grow to be solely privately financed.

A modified version of this strategy is to plan an expansion of a service beyond the capital city through a sector-based or key employer-based strategy. Jamaica cut the ribbon on its remodeled and modernized public employment service in Kingston in the fall of 2014 which has a more diversified, albeit limited, employment base (including information technology, health care, schools/universities). In 2015–16, as it planned to open offices in Montego Bay (tourism) and Manchester (agriculture-citrus, mining), it did so only through consultations and by signing agreements with the key business associations in these regions.

#3 Starting Specialized with Target Populations: Youth

In certain country contexts, the more pressing employment problem is with a sub-group of the labor force, often today large swaths of young people neither in the labor market nor school, a particularly large group in the Middle East, North Africa and key African countries. The strategy would be to build the core functions to start not for the whole working population but a target population, typically young people or women, for which there are specific labor market and placement needs. In Stage 1, however, great care must be taken as to whether a youth or any group-based core employment services center fits the problem. More often the employment barriers are multiple, not principally an issue of intermediation or information. In such cases, it is better to start with more integrated centers that combine on-the-job training, schooling, and then job placement to address multiple barriers together. These models are discussed in the next chapter as they are better suited to be linked at a later stage to a national employment service. To merit a specialized strategy in Stage 1, there must be a clear and fairly large cohort of jobs that fit the profile of the target group – entry-level jobs for youth, jobs adapted to persons with disabilities. As a strategy for starting in Stage 1, care must be taken so that a specialized center does not restrict the group's access to a wider range of jobs. More typically, specialized centers should be considered in Stage 2, providing specialized access and services to groups once a national database of jobs and a range of employer relationships have been developed. As an early strategy, Macedonia had a series of "tired" centers for receiving benefit claims which it converted into municipal youth centers that included job matching, mentoring and work skills training.

When the Strategy Doesn't Call for Employment Services If there is little private sector to consult with, or if employment conditions are dire, addressing the jobs problem may not include, or at least not put a priority on, creating Stage 1 employment services. This would be the case, for example, with countries with large rural workforces engaged in self-employment. In such countries, at best, employment services might play a purely sectoral role (just tourism, for example) which could be handled by stimulating or overseeing private provision. When the deficits are multiple and self-employment is the principal employer, far more comprehensive and integrated services would be more appropriate to start with. For those cases with a modicum of formal or at least urban employment, design features of core employment services would follow directly from the private sector strategy.

From Strategy to Key Design Features Just how the core services should be configured and delivered typically follows as an adaptation to the private sector jobs strategy. First, the "who": specifically, which employers, NGOs, and other institutions (such as cooperatives, voc-tech schools) need to be on board in this first stage to make the service viable, particularly who is willing to share costs, directly or in kind. Too many actors in Stage 1 are a recipe for hamstringing a service; networks for employment are better expanded and built over time. Partnering institutions and even staff need to be selected based on their ability to work with employers. Second, "what, where and how" involves adapting the three core services to the local market. These design decisions in the start-up phase should ideally be phased in, building, typically, from walk-in centers to outreach and satellite centers as demand builds. Some key operational decisions follow:

Operations/Mechanics for Stage One

Computerized Intake Systems In a computer age, the bare minimum management tool must be a computerized register of jobs and job seekers. Believe me, I have seen this still being done with paper, but never well. I have seen even more developing countries that have both – paper formats that they re-input various times into different computer programs. Even if it does not make sense to start off the service allowing job seekers to access the computer-based register system, paper-based systems cannot keep pace with the movement of jobs and job seekers.

For the registering of those seeking work, a basic set of indicators and a combination of self-registration and in-person registration have been the typical key elements of Stage 1. If the information requested is straight-forward enough, some self-registration for the computer-savvy job seeker can typically be part of an initial system. As far as possible, the job seeker register should be a set of simple key indicators (name, age, education profile, previous employment), saving more detailed information for the future development of the system, or a Part B for more skilled jobs when employer demand really merits it. What should be avoided from the outset is assigning job counselors the job of inputting basic information for those who need assistance; it is far more efficient to assign this inputting work to a receptionist/assistant. If the core employment service starts off with job counselors doing mostly administrative work, it can take years to redefine the job of the counselor in a walk-in service.

Many systems have begun without some form of number identification for the job seeker. Using standard national registry numbers (e.g. voter IDs, social security) if they exist, or developing one that coincides with another common form of assistance (like social services), enables a service to evolve over time to record the number of visits and types of services provided per client. I know this sounds basic but you have no idea how rarely this happens and how frustrating are the bureaucratic hurdles that can be in your way if this is attempted in Stage 2. Most developing countries err on the side of too much input information in Stage 1.

To make the register viable, provision is really needed to take people off who have either got work or are no longer looking for work. It sounds simple, but it's one of many of the fatal flaws of new systems, particularly if goals are set according to the number of job seekers enrolled; a better indicator of performance is number of jobs listed. A sunset provision is typically the easiest way to handle it – all job seekers must re-register after six or so months or they are eliminated.

For the register of jobs, the most success in listings has been obtained by those services that have provided or supported skilled staff to do this for firms, particularly in the first years of changing firms' attitudes about public listings. Many small and medium-sized businesses and even large employers in developing countries may have little experience of identifying the skills or tasks of a given job, and also fear an influx of job seekers. Some developing countries' services have included "job promotors" or business liaisons for this function, but equally useful is to train job counselors to work directly with employers to register jobs or periodically train association or other business personnel to do this. This helps strengthen job counselor contacts with local employers. Using some form of a "middleman" to gain job listings also helps firms learn from each other how to describe the positions to be filled and overcome misconceptions on the time needed to list vacancies.

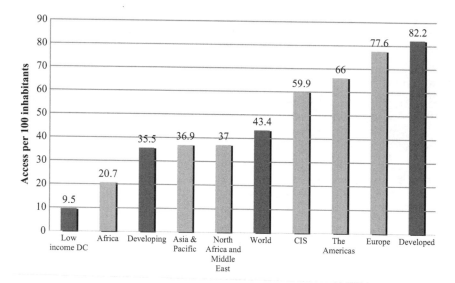

Graph 3.1 Proportion of individuals with internet access by region (% of population)
(Source: *The State of Broadband, 2015*, UNESCO-ITC. 2015 figures are estimated. CIS – Commonwealth of Independent States. Regions are based on the ITU BDT regions, see: http://www.itu.int/en/ITU-D/Statistics/Pages/definitions/regions.aspx)

In low internet usage countries (Graph 3.1), a country might only want self-registration to consist of basic information. Exceptions can be job fairs or other community meetings of job seekers and employers where self-registration can be easily supported. For developing countries, we call it an intake function, as typically an employee of the service is inputting data for either job openings or the profile of job seekers. Key here is the core service adapted to cultural norms and the rate of electronic literacy.

Initial Operational/Locational Set-Up

All Stage 1 services, if successful, expand into a wider range of walk-in, satellite, online, and co-located centers (with other services) in later stages. The first-stage decisions focus on how to deliver core services and where a service should be set up for a modern, depoliticized image with easy access for job seekers and employers.

Easy access for job seekers (close to public markets, other services) is typically not the same as easy access for employers (within their associations, at job fairs, through specialized contacts). If there are defined mechanisms to facilitate employer listings, then walk-in locations should really be oriented to public access. For public employment services in developing countries, one of the key fatal mistakes is to locate a service in an aging Ministry of Labor building (as they are owned by the government), particularly in the same building as the Ministry of Labor regulatory office. Nothing will discourage an employer from listing jobs more than the thought that it might prompt an inspector to visit their premises (the two functions need to be kept separate). In Panama City, the desks for the labor inspection service and the employment service were literally on two sides of the same large office until a major investment to expand the National Employment Service separated the two functions, with the result that job listings dramatically increased. Using isolated but less costly public ministry buildings may mean high transportation costs for the public to use the service – as happens, for example, with the cost of the bus service to reach the main National Employment Service office in Nassau, the Bahamas.[3]

Developing countries face inevitable fiscal constraints in leasing or buying facilities in populated areas, so a typical trade-off has been to locate administrative and central office staff in less accessible areas and use shared facilities (other Ministries, or the private sector) for satellite locations. Overall, little systematic study has been done to assist developing countries to analyze the factors involved in deciding how many offices to set up, where, when in the sequence of staged development, or the level of investment needed, particularly in an age of technology when online services can be considered an alternative to physical walk-in facilities. A summary of experience from developing countries in Stage 1 includes:

- Countries often locate "walk-in" services not by where traffic flows most normally, but where public agencies already own facilities. Countries should consider alternatives, including rental and shared spaces with other ministries if Ministry Offices are difficult to get to.
- At all costs countries should avoid locating walk-in employment centers in the same space as the Ministry of Labor's regulatory offices.
- There may be a tendency to overinvest in physical facilities that may be difficult to maintain over time. Better to identify the first set of centers in urban areas and complement this investment with rented facilities in satellite locations to await the growth of demand over time.
- Stage 1 countries should invest in a locational study/analysis before large investments in walk-in centers, taking into account maximizing convenience for job seekers and employers (e.g. located in city centers, shopping areas, near or within Chambers of Commerce, with easy access to public transportation) for urban areas first, and consider a more flexible approach to rural areas (e.g. mobile vans, shared facilities with local governments or the private sector). After well-established urban centers, the state employment service of Jalisco, on Mexico's west coast, invested in a mobile van which sets up shop in the main squares of more isolated communities on specific days of the week.

Building Competent Human Resources and a Depoliticized Foundation

The major public and private players creating a new core employment service face an ironic challenge – to avoid the politicized and non-competency-based hiring of the service's director and new staff – the very type of employment hiring it is trying to overcome in the economy! While political and business contacts and credibility are particularly important for the Center's Director, I have seen politicized hiring down to the job counselors and the administrative staff, all of whom are vulnerable to losing their jobs when a political or business leadership changes. This has been the biggest untold reason for the institutional failure of Stage 1 core employment services that I have seen. Hiring people with private sector experience, open competition for key posts, and regular training of staff can be critical in creating a depoliticized foundation for a Stage 1 service.

Legal/Regulatory Obstacles

In just a handful of developing countries, the creation of partnerships with private and non-profit organizations to reconfigure and relaunch a new form of Stage 1 core employment service may meet with legal prohibitions that must be addressed. The principal legal prohibitions are against for-profit firms operating and against sub-contracting by public entities. As well, Ministries of Labor charged with regulating private and non-profit firms and bureaucratic red tape have led to such partnerships being strangled out of business. There are unscrupulous firms taking advantage of workers which require regulation and oversight, but it can well be that the firms who need it most are not the ones being regulated! In Stage 1, the issue to be confronted is whether there are laws or regulations which will prohibit the operation of new institutional relationships beyond a public employment service monopoly.

Many (but not all) of these laws can trace their origins to an old International Labour Organization (ILO) Convention which prohibited private firms from charging for their services to workers. Eastern European and socialist countries (e.g. Cuba) had greater prohibitions on private sector activity of a more fundamental origin. The ILO has modernized greatly its approach to public-private partnerships in employment services, as evidenced from its newer Convention 197 that permits and regulates private employment agencies. Slowly countries have been either ignoring or removing legal prohibitions which mirrored these conventions, but this is not the case everywhere. Private employment agencies are still legally prohibited in Tunisia, for example.

Performance and Monitoring Indicators

Employing monitoring indicators from day one will help track the performance of a new service and keep future investments and time focused on better and better results. Too many performance and monitoring systems come later in a service's development, after inefficient processes, forms and work habits have become entrenched. Administrative data systems should be constructed to monitor the efficiency and effectiveness of the service, its local offices and their processes, including measurement of number of personnel attending clients, and number/type of clients. These systems can be expanded in Stage 2 to invest in more high-cost/high-yield tools once the basic model is consolidated. Particularly in Stage 1, keeping it simple enhances the ability of staff to see what works where quickly and minimizes bureaucratic burdens until the service is ready for a more extensive monitoring and evaluation framework that includes impact evaluations and cost-benefit analysis. These straightforward indicators include:

Stage 1: *Performance Indicators*

- Jobs listed: Number (and increase) in job vacancies registered.
- Placement rates: Percentage (as well as increase) in labor market insertion (job seekers in new employment supported by the employment service). Placement rates should be monitored by gender, ethnicity, education and income level as relevant to ascertain whether greater attention is needed for certain groups.[4]
- Quality of job attained: Salary[5] of new job compared to previous one or compared to a standard wage for new entrants.

Stage 1: *Monitoring Indicators* are used to inform and track performance, and can include:

- Number (or increase) in job seekers registered, to detect patterns and insure that registering job seekers is not outpacing job vacancy registration;
- Range of job vacancies registered (particularly higher-income and by sectors);
- Method used to register job vacancies (in person, on the phone, at job fairs) to help determine which are the most effective local methods to gain vacancies;
- Clients served per counselor.[6]

Stage 1: *Evaluation Types*

- Process evaluations;
- Administrative and systems evaluations, including comparing performance between regional offices or to national standards;
- Impact evaluations are feasible in early stages only in rare cases; typically impact evaluations for training programs run by core employment services can establish viable control groups in Stage 1.[7]

Drawing on International Technical Support There are now many international sources of technical support for the early building of labor intermediation services as jobs and workforce development have moved up the development food chain for most international organizations. The principal organizations providing specialized technical assistance for core employment services are (in alphabetical order): the Inter-American Development Bank (IDB), Labor Markets Unit; the International Labour Organization (ILO); the US Agency for International Development (USAID), Workforce Development Group; the World Association of Public Employment Services (WAPES); and the World Bank. National donor agencies also have special relationships with a core set of countries such as France in Northern Africa and Canada in Southeast Asia and the Caribbean.

Particularly for Stage 1, the most valuable sources of technical assistance and know-how can come from other developing countries and their networks of employment services. The World Association of Public Employment Services (WAPES) has most developed country members as well as developing country services from all regions of the world. The IDB created a network of public employment services now including 16 countries, termed *RED SEALC* (in English, Network of Employment Services from Latin America and the Caribbean). The network described in Box 3.2 sends teams from countries just starting up services to see other regional developing countries' systems or sends

---

Box 3.2 Neighbor-to-Neighbor: Advancing a Regional Technical Support Network in Employment Services

Officials from six Latin American public employment services had just finished touring the new facilities of the state public employment service in San Luis Potosí in North-Central Mexico. They sat down boisterously in the conference room, having just observed a new quality control process that invigorated staff and performance, brought in new employers in manufacturing, and won accolades among its peer state employment offices. They ended the study tour wrap-up meeting by telling the sponsoring Inter American Development staff that they wanted to create their own organization to see and learn from each other's experience. Among their

(continued)

Box 3.2 (continued)

peers, the exchange and the learning would be more real – they faced similar entrenched bureaucracies, skepticism from private employers, political shifts in public sector ministries, and difficulties getting resources and up-to-date technology.

Fast forward from that cathartic meeting in 2007 to today. RED SEALC (in Spanish, Network of Latin American and Caribbean Employment Services) was launched and now has 16 national public employment service members. Technical assistance goes two ways from a requesting country team: national employment services staff can observe other national services in action, and have sessions on applying innovations to their countries; or they can invite national or international experts to come and observe their services, making recommendations and working with local staff. Peruvian and Colombian teams visited Mexico's national employment service; an Estonian team came to the Bahamas. RED SEALC is managed for its member countries and technically supported by the Labor Markets Unit of the Inter-American Development Bank which has reached across the globe with other countries, Korea, Estonia and international partners, in particular, the World Association of Public Employment Services (WAPES), and the Organization of Economic Cooperation and Development (OECD) to expand neighbor-to-neighbor learning. For more information, see http://www.redsealc.netorwriteredsealc@iadb.org

experts to a country to help them implement or design systems at home. Particularly for developing countries which share similar roadblocks – private sector companies which won't initially return their calls, politicization of employment, frequently changing political parties that pull out resources – the visual stimulus of seeing a labor intermediation service which has managed to overcome such obstacles in a few short years can be a key change agent. Technical visits have helped a number of developing countries leap over old, hardened practices to make substantial gains in just a few years.

SOME STAGE 1 INNOVATIONS

Job Fairs

One-day job fairs are held widely, by the most rudimentary to the most sophisticated labor intermediation services. In Stage 1, job fairs are typically low-cost, open-air one-day events held in town centers. One can visualize: open tables of employers conducting interviews; schools and NGOs soliciting trainees or participants in programs leading to jobs; on site workshops for job hunters; and possibly access to computers to register for services or search for employment. The innovation for Stage 1 countries comes in their strategic use to: (1) promote and change the image of a service bringing it directly to new users; (2) provide on-the-spot,one-day placement interviews with employers who may be hard to reach or not yet ready to formally list their jobs with a service; (3) provide linkages to other local services before the service itself would be able to systematically provide referrals to other programs; and, (4) provide a "walk-by" showcase of core services to populations who might not typically be aware of such services.

As far as possible, Stage 1 countries should view these job fairs as part of their regular operations. This means that both jobs offered and job seekers are registered into the national register, with particular follow-up right at the fair. While job fairs are relatively efficient for one-day job matching, many services neglect to keep track of who might have been offered work via a job fair, thus underestimating the job placement rates of a service as well as limiting information on what or who has been successful (or not) via job fairs.

As a service evolves towards a labor intermediation service, Stage 1 job fairs – inviting all employers in a regional area – can evolve to different strategic or themed job fairs as outreach to new employers and different types of job seekers. The State Employment Service in Yucatán, Mexico, for example, had a large university population that was not connecting to local employers in science and technology despite demand for these young workers. A specialized job fair was held for young people in these key sectors in the modern convention center as neither high tech employers nor young people would likely have passed by the walk-in center at the municipal building.[8] Mexico, now well into Stage 2, created in later years "virtual" job fairs to attract tech-savvy youth while at the same time running specialized and general job fairs throughout the country.

Training Programs Building to Stage 1

With a crisis in youth employment, a number of Latin American and Caribbean countries first built demand-based youth training programs, and then used this platform to rebuild their public employment services, integrating them with the youth training model. The renovated public employment service then had a ready stream of young people entering its offices and new relationships with local employers to expand its listings for adults. The Latin American youth training model, starting first in Chile, combines classroom-based and on-the-job training by contracting out to private providers who have incentives to insure a high percentage of young people get employed afterwards. Its different versions have been closely studied for their effectiveness.[9] David Card and Jochen Kluve note that this youth training model works better in a developing country context than other youth training models in the industrialized world. This new type of training innovation was introduced in environments when employers rarely openly competed positions and where few risked hiring young people from disadvantaged neighborhoods; these one- to three-month on-the-job traineeships also served as a trial work period, prying open vacancies that did not technically exist before the trial. These programs both built new relationships with employers and brought young people, typically up to 26 years old, through the doors of employment services looking not for work but for paid training. Incentives were created to make a match in job placement not through personal contacts, but by giving employer and disadvantaged youth a one- to three-month supervised job trial/training period in which to develop or demonstrate good work skills.

The Dominican Republic provides a key example. Only after the success of its youth training program *Empleo y Juventud* (Employment and Youth) had achieved high placement rates for youth, did the public sector, working with employers, invest in a modernization of the public employment service – computers, new offices, a linked job network – all of which provided a more modern platform not only for the youth program but also for the previously moribund public employment service. The Dominican Republic's national employment service could then re-establish Stage 1 core services with management of youth training placements to a larger network and menu of employment and training services.

The Tech Revolution: What Stage 1 Role?

Computers and now the internet, social media and cell phones have clearly brought innovations in the delivery and management of core employment services – in all stages. To name but a few changes: computerized and online management systems; text messages to make appointments and receive job listings; job announcements on Facebook; and job search and career courses you can take online. Even the most tech-savvy countries, however, rely on person-to-person services. Walk-in and person-to-person services even if by telephone are vital, particularly for the poor and those without access to or familiarity with the internet.

In Stage 1, as a service first tries to engage job seekers and employers, great care is needed to employ technology judiciously and strategically and not get ahead of the client or neglect established patterns for job connections. There should be a distinction in Stage 1 between employing technology for systems used by management versus systems used by would-be clients. There is no dispute that the management system, specifically the job and job seeker registers, must be computerized. Without a computerized job bank, a service cannot update quickly as jobs are filled nor manage growth in the client base. But neither job seekers or employers are typically ready in Stage 1 for all job matching to be done only by searching a database or for 100% self-registration to be required of job seekers and employers. Graph 3.1 demonstrates the wide differences among developing regions in the use of the internet by individuals, expressed as a percentage of 100 individuals. The disparity in individual use of the internet by region and by level of development in 2015 is striking.

While 82% of individuals in the developed world have access to the internet, the percentage for developing countries is less than half of that, at 35%. The disparity *among* developing countries is even greater – less than 10% of people living in low-income countries have such access[10] while high-income developing/emerging countries like Singapore and Qatar have among the highest rates worldwide (88% and 98% respectively). The lowest rates of access are recorded throughout Africa (20.7%) as well as in select countries of the Asia-Pacific region, such as Myanmar (2.1%), Timor-Leste (1.2%), and Afghanistan (6.4%), with only 37% on average.[11] Higher average rates are found in the Americas and the countries of the CIS (Commonwealth of Independent States), Russia and former Soviet/Eurasian countries.[12]

Given the wide variance in availability of technology, it is easy and common for the job placement and registration function to start off maladapted to countries' population and labor market, greatly restricting access for those who most need it. If cultural norms to register jobs openly are not yet well-established, self-registration by businesses will reach a quick plateau and could quickly discourage job seekers from returning a second time to a service with outdated vacancies, listings not accurately portraying jobs, or vacancies that get no response. If the job-matching process is also exclusively self-serve, meaning the job seeker looks for jobs online and contacts firms themselves, businesses will soon get discouraged by receiving too many poorly qualified applicants and may never get the technical support they need to open up the best jobs to public listings.

A number of Middle East and African nations may already be getting the reputation of rushing to put their services online without developing an efficient in-person set of services first. This may lead to a set of services only relevant to the most educated, as in the case of the Middle East – where only the most educated 37% of the population uses the internet. How widely technology is available and accessible to majority and minority groups should guide its use in client-driven services in Stage 1. It should never, however, be to the exclusion of building a foundation of person-to-person matching and direct contacts with employers oriented to creating a new, more open and transparent system of job search and intermediation.

Mobile Units/Rural Adaptations

Innovating for rural areas has become more common once an urban core employment service has gotten off the ground. If the goal is to enable rural workers to access a national job register and reliable connectivity is not an issue, creating internet-based satellite stations in rural community centers, private internet cafes, schools with training of local personnel for oversight could be an option in Stage 1. Mobile vans which have been used in places like Jalisco, Mexico to bring a complete set of core employment services and counselors to different hard-to-reach communities represent a relatively small investment that could be applied to a Stage 1 service. Local employers could be enticed to join in a rural job fair, but such fairs should also be widened to bring in local NGO programs that have productive sector and agricultural support programs in the region. One of the many challenges of rural self-employment is that it is rarely sustainable full-time in one sector only (e.g. just farming, fishing). One role of rural employment-targeted initiatives would be to demonstrate a range of viable sectors and bring together entrepreneurs. As discussed next in Chapter 2, however, comprehensive support to microentrepreneurs requires more sustained and diverse support, from technical to marketing to credit. This is more than a modified urban employment services model could reasonably deliver. In particularly low-income, highly rural economies, it is likely best to separate out urban from rural employment services models in the earliest stages so that the appropriate mix of services develops. Coordination and linkage can advance more naturally as each more tailored service matures.

Start in Employment Crisis Mode

Impact evaluations and common sense have taught that core employment services work better when an economy is growing. This makes sense: more jobs mean more ability to place un or underemployed people. Yet a developing country irony (or reality, one could argue) is that a number of the

Box 3.3 Growing from Crisis Mode: South Korea's Rapid Transition out of Stage 1

In one year, 1998, South Korea, a country long accustomed to a stable employment environment, found itself in the midst of a true employment crisis. Official unemployment went from 2% to 8% in that year as part of a financial crisis that spread through East Asia. The Korean Public Employment Service existed, but had such a poor image with both employers and now the newly unemployed that it barely served as a good conduit for new unemployment insurance claims, let alone having the job listings and services to lead people out of the crisis.

Sang Hyon Lee recalls they had to "change the deep-rooted bad image" of the service in order to entice employers back into listing openings as the crisis eased and get job seekers to come in. The South Korean government invested in new more modern walk-in centers, more like walking into a business center than a public office. They promoted the new service widely, in subways and in public places. The public employment service moved from 99 job centers

(continued)

> **Box 3.3** (continued)
>
> in 1998 to 168 in 2001, then dropping down to 82 in 2008 as the service evolved into online access and unemployment levels eased.
>
> In the times of high unemployment, middle-aged men were the principal clients, whereas today the case load has multiplied and diversified. By 2009, Korea had fully entered a new advanced Stage 2 role and created a tailored support program for low-income job seekers. It has created a new information platform, the Korean Employment Information Service, connected now with municipal job centers and special job centers for the disabled.
>
> Note: Based on presentation by Sang Hyon Lee at Seminar on Performance Management, March 18, 2015.

now best developing country labor intermediation services had their start in Stage 1 when unemployment was at crisis levels. It was the political need and political will to direct resources to combat climbing unemployment that prompted countries like Korea and Mexico to create or renovate their national employment services. Both these systems stayed in Stage 1 for only one year and were then able to adapt their services to respond to economic growth as their respective crises were eased. Sang Hyon Lee of Korea's public employment service recalls that Korea had a moribund service until national attention focused on employment in the 1998 financial crisis.[13] The Korean case as described in Box 3.3 demonstrates how important a different image and political attention to employment were in building the foundation for a now comparatively large national intermediation service.

While the routes to rethink Stage 1 are diverse among developing and now emerging and advanced economies, employment dynamics in today's economies have compelled new public-private-non-profit platforms to enable basic employment services to grow into labor intermediation services in Stage 2. The traditional model of relying solely on a small public employment service to grow by public investment fits neither highly constrained developing country budgets nor developing economies with more diverse employment needs.

Moving Onto Stage 2

If core employment services get rolling in Stage 1 in a flexible model with private sector participation, my personal observation is that developing countries can move fairly quickly from delivering the core job register, counseling and placement services into the next stage of adding or connecting to a wider range of services as a labor intermediation service. Developing countries quickly confront a diverse client base with multiple barriers to employment, including where they live (locational), what skills they have (or don't have), and whether their education is adequate for the job market. Very early into Stage 1, employment services will confront face education and training systems that produce few graduates ready to be matched immediately to jobs. Fundamental institutional weaknesses in education and training is why so many developing country employment services need to connect to or manage themselves "intermediary" services in Stage 2 that better prepare and enable some of these "not ready" for primetime job seekers to transition to work.

Failure – or, just as common, fits and restarts – can also happen in Stage 1. Despite its success and innovation, Honduras' new service found itself temporarily stalled in a political presidential cycle. Even if successful, a Stage 1 service can still lose funding or personnel, for a host of reasons, only to be restarted a few months or even years later. This is a more fundamental institutional problem of development, but it again argues for developing basic core services with employer support and diverse funding sources. At best, this book can serve as a guide to weathering storms by demonstrating what can be achieved by building from a solid base and then adapting quickly to local economic needs, advancing to the more institutionally stable Stage 2.

Employment services are not immune from the fundamental institutional and economic challenges that affect sectors from education to health care to agricultural development. This book intends to show by example that this up-and-down history can be modified and even overcome by adapting better public and private roles to challenging employment contexts.

Just a final note on the application of employment to labor intermediation services in conflict and former conflict zones. While these are clearly the areas in employment crisis, the core employment service models discussed here are most relevant to start in Stage 1 in urban areas that have a minimum cohort of formal employment, connecting with rural areas as the services consolidate into Stage 2, as rural areas typically require a more integrated set of services oriented to self-employment. Improving employment in conflict zones is a very special and difficult case – first, if the conflict is ongoing, and second, if the post-conflict environment has created large fissures across the public and private sectors and within a geographic zone. In such cases, core employment services cannot begin as a set of core services; they must start as part of a wider delivery of social, economic and employment services, more appropriately discussed in Chapter 5 where more integrated models are discussed.

NOTES

1. "Total Labor Force: 2004", World Bank Jobs Database, http://data.worldbank.org/indicator/SL.TLF.TOTL.IN?page=2.
2. Jacqueline Mazza, "Labor Intermediation Services: Lessons for Latin America and the Caribbean," 2003.
3. New investments in the Bahamas National Employment Service are intended to add more accessible offices in both Nassau and the Family Islands.
4. Many Stage 1 employment services seek to measure labor market insertion rates before building the administrative data and follow-up mechanisms to do this accurately, thereby underestimating both the direct and indirect impact of the service. Also underestimated are indirect impacts of services, for example, those who saw announcements which led to placement.
5. Ascertaining the improvement (or not) in salary is the best proxy for job quality but can be difficult to verify and track, particularly with so many informal jobs. It may be that this indicator awaits Stage 2 when either follow-up processes for job placement are systematized or links are made with social security systems (best-case scenario) to verify automatically by worker ID number.
6. Assumes that administrative systems assign clients to counselors, typical in advanced countries but less so in developing countries. If the service is not yet run under a case management system (typically a Stage 2 innovation), the number of job seekers to number of job counselors by walk-in office or other method can be tracked.
7. The amount of experimentation needed to build to sufficient scale with reliable input data in Stage 1 often means the model to be evaluated and the ability to construct a viable control group are not consolidated until Stage 2.
8. Christina Kappaz and Rosa Cavallo, "Case Studies: Mexican Public Employment Service", 2009.
9. Pablo Ibarraran and David-Rosas Shady, "Evaluating the Impact of Job Training Programs in Latin America: Evidence from IDB Funded Operations," 2009.
10. Country data was organized by income level and region according to World Bank classifications.
11. *The State of Broadband 2015*, Annex 6, http://www.itu.int/ict/statistics.
12. *Ibid.*
13. Sang Hyon Lee, comments at Seminar on Performance Management, March 18, 2015.

CHAPTER 4

Stage 2: From Employment to Labor Intermediation Services

The traditional employment services model that grew up in the advanced economies in the 1940s–60s had it much easier compared to today's developing and emerging economies. They only had to work marginally well because so many employment-school-work connections happened outside the employment services model. They had relatively reliable sources of public financing, job change was less frequent, and most employment was formal and largely industrial. Post-WWII advanced countries expanded via public financing, as their costs to benefit were largely measured by reducing claims on generous unemployment insurance.

Growing from a core set of employment services into a wider, more efficient range of services that fit more diverse developing economies operating in a more global world means thinking very differently about what services are needed, who provides them and how they are provided. Three "big-picture" changes form the heart of advancing to Stage 2 in a more global era when the public sector cannot do it all and the employment problems come from multiple sources. This chapter lays out these three broad changes while describing under each a host of different routes, programs and ideas tested by country experience.

The first big-picture change is that core employment services need to grow quickly by adding an extended set of labor intermediation services that fit the national economy. Second, to accomplish the leap forward from core employment to labor intermediation services requires attention to greater efficiency and better performance, using management

© The Author(s) 2017
J. Mazza, *Labor Intermediation Services in Developing Economies*,
DOI 10.1057/978-1-137-48668-4_4

restructuring, case management and other innovations of the core public-private-NGO service. The third big-picture change is supporting and even monitoring the functioning and growth of the wider intermediation market – thinking about building the range of private, public, non-profit organizations, and schools that can form a national intermediation system here called "Jobs Inc." Your grandfather's public employment services never had to think about the importance of both enlarging the pie and making a better one, in which job and school transitions are more frequent and need to function more smoothly. Do not despair if this sounds too complicated! Stage 2 is already under way in strange unlikely places in the developing world! It is a gradual process of evolution, not a big bang!

STARTING IN OR GROWING INTO STAGE 2

Stage 2 can and has been launched from two distinct starting points in developing countries. It can grow, as this book lays out, from a small, newly-created Stage 1 model of public-private cooperation in employment services, building from this core base of services. It can also be launched from an existing, mid-size foundation of a functioning public employment service and/or a base of firms, NGOs, and placement agencies already doing employment services work. Middle- and high-income developing countries, including much of the Middle East, North Africa, Eastern Europe and Eurasia, typically fit in this second category.

Are there indicators of whether a country has achieved the institutional foundation needed to launch Stage 2? While not at all a science, there are institutional characteristics that can help assess readiness. Readiness in this case means that the core employment matching and listing is functioning at a level that makes it possible for the administrative model to expand into new services while still improving core functions (job listings, placement). I have seen remodeled public employment services try to add many new services too soon, thereby losing the confidence of employers, straining staff, and ultimately delivering on neither core nor new extended services. If a country has begun in Stage 1, typically with a new public-private partnership, it should have at least a year of operation delivering core services and potentially one related service (the Dominican Republic, for instance, had at least three years with its youth training program). The placement rate of a core service, including placement via training, should hopefully exceed 30% before embarking on adding new services.

In the case of countries with a pre-existing foundation of institutions, the public employment service must be operating at functional levels of job placement – that is, a minimum of 20% of those who register for jobs receive them under the service. I have not yet seen Stage 2 launched solely as a set of private sector firms and NGOs without the public sector, but it is feasible; to do so one would imagine there must already be some form of linkage or inter-institutional cooperation already operating.

Some existing public employment services, particularly in the Middle East and Eastern Europe, may have a mission that is not principally job placement in the private sector. They may principally be registering citizens for government benefits or maintaining a register of those awaiting public sector jobs (Egypt, for example). If such a service does not yet have the private sector links to place more than 20% of job seekers in jobs, than a Stage 1 shake-up of the institutional framework and a new image is likely needed. These largely middle- and high-income countries with a functioning institutional base can utilize management restructuring (big-picture item number 2) to essentially reconfigure the kind of public-private partnership needed to create labor intermediation services, short-circuiting the need to return to Stage 1.

Size actually doesn't matter much to start Stage 2 as expansion of the client base is typically an output of the investments in Stage 2. What is essential as a foundation is a functional public-private or private-NGO set of core services that can launch an expansion of coverage and effectiveness. Stage 2 can, for example, be launched (and has been) with a functional base of institutions only in the capital city, as expansion can be designed to link the model to employment centers outside the capital city or to facilitate internal mobility. It is in the expansion of coverage, effectiveness and utility to a country-specific set of jobs deficits that we see even further variation among developing countries and use of high-income country instruments. This adaption over time to the national labor market begins with the first big-picture change to add new or linked services.

BUILDING TO A LABOR INTERMEDIATION SERVICE: CREATING AND LINKING NEW SERVICES

Core employment services, while important to do efficiently to establish a service, will soon face limitations in developing country markets, both in relation to dysfunctions present in the local labor market and in getting new job listings where formal sectors are small. Perhaps it will seem that there are not enough jobs to list or employers will say they can't find qualified workers or don't want to take risks making new hires. Extended services are used to help pry open job markets further, to address multiple barriers to employment, and in doing so build a basic employment service into a labor intermediation service. Particularly for developing countries this can extend the reach of the service into more "hidden" employment markets – such as internal and external migration, training leading to employment, and self-employment.

These additional services are called in this book "extended services" because they go beyond traditional matching of job seekers to vacancies of an employment service to extend the reach, effectiveness and relevance of the service. These extended services can either be delivered by the new public-private service or linked through information or referral, or contracted to independent providers. Extended services are grouped into three types in this book as a way of highlighting the distinct methods by which they seek to improve reach, relevance and effectiveness:

- **Information Services (Type 1)** – these services provide data/information on labor market and career trends and, in some cases, information on the availability and performance of training and educational institutions so that job seekers can make better job search, career planning, training or education decisions based on employment prospects.
- **"Intermediation Plus" Services (Type 2)** – these are services that either lead directly to a job match at the end or put the job seeker on the road to a job. Most common are skills or employment-readiness training designed so that trainees are placed either directly in jobs or that lead to jobs in the near future. Other forms of "intermediation plus" services include screening, testing, and profiling employees, acting as an in-house human resources department. The term "intermediation plus" services is used for a reason in this book: to deter the adoption of a range of services that are not focused or directly linked to employment and maintain a razor-sharp focus on delivering connections to employment. When there are multiple and complex barriers to employment involved, this book argues they are best handled by specialized programs targeting disadvantaged groups.
- **Program Administration and Support Services (Type 3)** – here delivery of employment services is combined with other related labor

market and social programs in order to draw more potential clients through the door and improve the administration and coordination of labor market or social programs.

Before getting overwhelmed by the range of services, please remember that Stage 2 means building services selectively over time, with emphasis on both *building* and *selectivity*. Particularly when one employs the third big-picture perspective on the whole intermediation market, no one public provider could or should do it all. Each of the services listed below are found in the spectrum of developing countries up to the middle- and high-income developing nations. Each country presents a different configuration of public and private institutions that might be drawn in to be principal providers or partners in such services. By Stage 2, we are far distant from the model of a single publically financed employment service trying to do it all. For each of the following extended services, one can name developing country cases where a public-private service provides it itself, contracts it to an external provider, or links to or relies principally on an outside provider to fill the market niche. These "no-one-size-fits-all" configurations in developing countries come about for many reasons – national and local institutional strengths and weaknesses, erratic funding cycles, capacities built during employment emergencies. Each of the extended services is described in this first section on creating and linking new services. Which services are created and which are linked via a network or referral is part of a larger alchemy laid out in the final section of this chapter. They are listed as the first big-picture change as typically a few new services are introduced on the road to realizing that, to grow and diversify more, the now labor intermediation service will need management restructuring (big picture item #2) to advance further.

Table 4.1 provides an summary of the three types of extended services. Next follows a fuller explanation of specific services under each of the three types, all of which have taken form in developing countries, adapted in different combinations, configurations and strengths to very different labor markets. If one were to generalize, nearly all Stage 2 services develop an early base of labor market information (Type 1) as this serves the information needs for better job hunting and better service delivery, and either link or manage a skills training program (Type 2) as this is an area of such fundamental deficit in the developing world.

Table 4.1 Extended service types

Extended service types	Service description	Principal client
Information services (Type 1)	Labor market observatory/ information systems	Job seekers, employers, educational and training institutions
	Training, microenterprise, education information systems	Students/trainees, institutions, private providers
"Intermediation Plus" (Type 2)	Management of training or other active labor market instruments	Employers; workers; job seekers
	Migrant support services	Internal & external migrants; employers
	Microenterprise/self-employment support	Self-employed
	Placement and human resources services for employers	Employers
Program administration and support services (Type 3)	Labor market/unemployment insurance administration	Eligible unemployed, workers
	Social service gateway/referral	Eligible population

TYPE 1: INFORMATION SERVICES

Labor Market Information Observatories and Employment Portals (Type 1)

The advent of the computer and internet age has led to important leaps to information systems that can track key employment trends, indicating where jobs, wages and investments are growing. Online labor market information is today still more prevalent in middle-income economies, but they become even more feasible for lower-income economies once basic labor market surveying is in place. Today *labor market information systems* are more commonly called labor market "observatories" as they are watching employment trends in a given nation. They disaggregate employment trends by sex, age, location, and sector as well as by wage trends. Mexico and Chile have among the more sophisticated online observatories in the developing world. You can find consolidated labor market observatories of job listings and labor market studies online for Syria as well (www.lmo.sy). Less than a decade ago, labor market information would be used only by labor economists to write academic papers on labor market trends. Today's observatories are put online with more practical purposes in mind – providing job seekers, training and educational institutions with information on employment trends to aid better decision-making in career choices for job seekers and in aligning curriculums and training to areas in which both jobs and wages are growing.

The labor market data to construct observatories typically comes from quarterly or annual labor force surveys, as employment trends change so quickly that census data every ten years is useful only for the broadest trends. It is helpful, but not essential, if a labor intermediation service is the one conducting the surveys, but more often than not, this capacity rightly lies in national statistical institutes. National quarterly labor force surveys are unfortunately not the norm, particularly in low-income developing nations, but should be the goal. With weaknesses in labor force or household survey data, many labor intermediation services draw on business and economic surveys, as well as commission their own specialized surveys through universities or firms. Intermediation services are typically better equipped to survey their users and to conducted specialized surveys. The use of labor market information systems by job seekers, employers, and training and educational institutions is facilitated by another trend: "co-locating" this online data with an employment portal – a website containing online job registers, job-seeking tools and other information for job seekers. Most developing country labor market observatories I know started as separate systems and, when ready, joined forces with employment portals for wider access and impact. Nepal has specialized labor market information focused on foreign employment. The Foreign Employment Promotion Board is "mandated to carry out studies of international labour markets" and to "collect, process and publish information that promote specific jobs" while its parent agency, the Department of Foreign Employment, regulates and licenses recruitment agencies, mostly in the Persian Gulf and East Asia.[1]

Employment portals are becoming more and more comprehensive in both developed and middle-income developing countries. As just mentioned, they are one central web address or location that hosts a national job register for online job search, but then extend much further with icons and links to other job registries (e.g. private agencies, local business associations), online job search information and training, career-planning tools, and local labor market information. Poland's employment observatory contains job availability, wages, career information and hiring expectations.[2] Co-location on one web site is the most common format, but advances are taking place. Only a few advanced country systems and industries have converted labor market and career information into one entry portal – that is, with a click on a career or job type you can see the trends in the career, job types that lead you through a career path, and available job vacancies corresponding to that career path. New Zealand's career development system (careersnz.com) and that of the Hospitality Guild of the United Kingdom are the wave of the future!

Training, Microenterprise and Higher Education Information Systems (Type 1)

Another type of information system catalogues employment-related programs – describing available programs, costs, time frame and, with luck, information on success rates. Program information databases are typically separated by type; this could include available local programs by training field, types and availability of microenterprise support programs, as well as, for higher education, program, graduation and employment rates. Information databases on programs are, admittedly, more frequently compiled in the advanced countries, and, in higher education, maintained more on a voluntary basis by universities or university associations themselves.

For labor intermediation services, systematic databases of available training programs by field and microenterprise programs are particularly important as a service moves to serve individual clients on a case management basis (see next Type 2 service). Developing countries in particular often find themselves with a web of uncoordinated interventions with different donor-financing sources, particularly for the poor or disadvantaged groups. Donors make various attempts to create inventories of programs, but there is rarely a central information database regularly updated. With such databases, labor intermediation services can also market themselves as a provider for screening, profiling and referring candidates to employment-related programs (see human resource services).

TYPE 2: SERVICES AND PROGRAMS TO SUPPORT EMPLOYMENT

Training and Other Active Labor Market Programs (Type 2)

For good reason, the most sought-after and typical service linked with a core employment service is training. In today's global labor market, employers are expressing greater concern worldwide about the lack of both technical and life skills, the latter also called "soft" or life skills with technical skills being "hard" skills. As an active labor market policy, good design, linkage to employers, and on-the-job "on site" training are known to improve what can be the modest results of training. From impact evaluations and study, we know that many training programs can cost a lot and have little to no impact; even well-designed training has been shown to have its impact principally in the medium term.[3] But the skills and basic education deficits are much greater for many more people in developing countries and there is rightfully an emphasis on experimentation with training models for different developing country contexts that get better results. Many argue, with evidence, that good training may be more effective in developing countries if a skills gap is a particularly binding constraint on getting hired.[4]

National public and public-private intermediation services are playing a key role in this experimentation either in managing such training, providing incentives for firms (e.g. subsidies to trainees), linking trainees with firms, or creating referral systems that demonstrate which training programs result in jobs at the end. In whatever country context, research is clear that training on the job, or led, designed and operated by firms gets the best results.[5]

Particularly in developing countries where there is such poor articulation of skill needs combined with poor schooling, labor intermediation services can be seen as a key channel to bring training closer to labor market demand. They are best suited to work with firms on "intermediation plus"-type training – that is, short-term training whose objective is job placement. This is the model pursued by most public employment services in Latin America and the Caribbean, but the Middle East emphasizes classroom-based training without much monitoring and evaluation of placement results as found in Lebanon, Syria, Egypt and Jordan.[6] Turkey's public employment agency (known by its initials ISKUR) introduced job and vocational counselors together with expanding the coverage and quality of vocational training.[7] In Bolivia, the public employment service places young people in firms for up to three months of training (paying them a transport and living subsidy) and then measures and monitors how many get hired either in the same or another firm. Turkey jump-started an expansion of what they termed vocational training (three months of skills training)[8] growing from 30,000 traineeships in 2008 to 464,000 in 2012 to accompany labor market reforms. ISKUR managed some of this training directly; other traineeships were contracted out to private providers. With World Bank support, Turkey conducted a comprehensive impact evaluation of its large program. It was the first evaluation for a developing country which included looking three years later at labor market impacts. The evaluation found significant impact on formal employment over the first year, but that impact unfortunately dissipated over the three years. They did find that the training had stronger impacts when delivered by private providers, but even private providers struggled to demonstrate the impact of such training on labor market outcomes.[9]

"Intermediation plus"-type training for developing countries is for those closest to job ready. Even here, the development field is just beginning to explore whether other modifications of instruments, such as very short work orientation leading to job placement (less than a month), job shadowing, work/study, and mentoring, can be even less costly and potentially as effective for job placement as 3–6 month training programs. In South Africa, the International Youth Foundation is working with young people on "learningships." In Riviera Maya, Mexico, the local Hotel Association, working with a local vocational-technical institution, developed a range of tools and new career-track curriculums to begin to shift to greater hiring of upper secondary students when this applicant pool had previously been considered not job ready (Box 5.1). Any of these "intermediation plus" instruments requires a good assessment of which candidates need such short-term training or work orientation, comprising largely basic work skills orientation, to facilitate placement, and which job seekers need far more sustained interventions.

While training is the best known active labor market policy instrument, there are a few others which can and have been managed by labor intermediation services. Remember active labor market policies are incentives to enable workers to actively insert themselves into or stay in a job. The two other principal active instruments employed in developing countries are wage subsidies and temporary employment. Wage subsidies partially subsidize a worker's wage as an incentive for an employer to hire someone they might not have normally hired (for example, a person with disabilities, someone with a criminal record, or long-term unemployed) or to keep a person from being laid off, usually at a time of economic crisis. Wage subsidies have been shown to be effective in some contexts. While training is typically the predominant active labor market program, wage subsidies are utilized more as employment incentives in Middle Eastern and North African countries for young entrants – for example, in Jordan, Morocco and Tunisia.[10] They are used to facilitate recruitment of targeted populations who might otherwise be overlooked. Temporary employment, short-term jobs or community jobs, typically at a minimum salary for one to three months, actually have a poor record for helping someone get an actual job later.[11] They are more appropriate as income support in times of crisis, as used during financial crises in East Asia[12] and in Haiti following the 2010 earthquake.

There are many other types of training designed to address greater skills deficits, requiring longer-term interventions; also included should be the reform of vocational-technical high schools which around the developing world constitute a glaring deficit for preparing the future workforce. Apprenticeships of one to two years have had great success in countries like Germany and Austria, but how to adapt these, and with which sectors or private firms in more challenging developing country markets is still being explored. In building cost-effective training services in Stage 2, this book argues for emphasis first on the type of training for which labor intermediation services are best suited. This requires direct relationships with the private sector (or informal workplaces), strict monitoring and evaluation, and continual experimentation with instruments to keep the programs/incentives focused on the impact on job placement. Special consideration and different programs are needed for populations facing more complex and multiple barriers to employment (see next section).

Programs for Disadvantaged Groups: Special Considerations (Type 2)

One of the most important and challenging problems in developing countries is how to put disadvantaged populations on a path out of poverty to good jobs. The advanced countries as well are still struggling with how to do this. These are populations with multiple barriers to employment, ones that cannot be adequately addressed in short periods with services ending in a job. They often require daily interventions and supportive living environments. The diverse challenges are great: young people living in slums; isolated indigenous peoples; women in restrictive cultures. Barriers are multiple, individual and societal: basic literacy/education deficits, criminal records or crime-filled neighborhoods, drug or alcohol addiction, labor market or social discrimination. As these are some of the neediest populations, there is a tendency, particularly for public employment services, to design specialized interventions to run simultaneously with services for those who have far fewer barriers to entering the labor market.

I am going to say something controversial here. Jobs programs or services that require daily follow-up, changed environments (e.g. Jobs Corps facilities away from home environments as in the United States, Youth Build programs in developing countries), and multiple specialized interventions (e.g. drug rehabilitation, counseling, job readiness skills) are best managed by specialized non-governmental organizations in developing countries. This is not to say there are not important provisions to improve access for special populations to labor intermediation services, such as wheelchair access in a modern service center catering to persons with disabilities in

Michoacán, Mexico, or specialized employment centers in Tunisia. Labor intermediation services can also be good "connectors" of social and labor market services (see Type 3). But if we are talking about sustained interventions leading to employment, non-governmental organizations more often have the capability for daily oversight of multiple interventions over longer periods combined with knowledge of local community environments and financing to permit experimentation. In these cases, labor intermediation services are better suited to refer candidates to such programs and even contract specialized interventions (as Australia has done). Job placement can then be embedded and sequenced in with addressing multiple barriers – for youth, for example, with developing self-esteem, life skills, motivation, and technical skills. There is much discussion in development today with advancing life or employability skills for youth and disadvantaged populations; learning how to do this is still a work in progress.

Specialized programs and providers have the advantage of being able to test out models over time tailored to multiple barriers in different developing country contexts. Innovation can flourish in such tailored environments. As youth is a particular concern in much of the developing world, here are mentioned two very different approaches for out-of-school young people from poor neighborhoods. First, from the dangerous slums of Rio de Janeiro, Brazil, came *Galpão Aplauso* in Portuguese, a non-governmental-private-sector youth training program with a theatre arts focus. Impact evaluations have shown positive impacts on job placement, but intermediation is not done by electronic matching, but by one woman (or in the future a man!) who uses her own contacts to prod employers to take a chance on a young person she can personally vouch for, and whom she will personally support in the transition to employment. A second youth multi-intervention program all over the developing world is Youth Build International, described in Box 4.1. "Embedded intermediation" carried out for disadvantaged youth by the International Youth Foundation (www.iyf.org) also does not look anything like the classic active labor market policy of employment services, nor should it. Labor intermediation services should be aware that in key cases separate, more specialized intervention is superior, particularly when groups need far more sustained support leading up to and *during* employment. Labor intermediation services can play important linkage roles, incorporating recruitment through their job fairs and referral information systems, providing links with interested employers, but in these specialized cases the intermediation function – supporting the program recipient into a job – is embedded within the program itself.

Box 4.1 Building Life and Job Skills in Poor Neighborhoods: Youth Build goes International and to South Africa
Youth Build started in the United States with young people on the margins: high school dropouts, many with criminal records, all from poor neighborhoods where careers in the drug trade are the norm. Youth Build engages young people full-time in community building projects combined with basic schooling. Some Youth Build projects are actually charter high schools. Young people may repair homes of the elderly, rebuild sidewalks or community centers – not necessarily with the goal of entering the construction trades, although some do. The construction skills are used to build what today are called life skills: self-esteem, teamwork, social-emotional skills, observing workplace rules. Youth Build has moved globally, implementing country-adapted models with local NGOs. You can find community-based projects in more than 12 countries reaching Israel, Iraq, Peru, Haiti, Bosnia, and Bulgaria as well as South Africa. South Africa incorporated the Youth Build model into its Youth Ministry in 2008, concentrating on engaging young people to build community housing. Youth Build-South Africa is now training 1400 young people in 13 separate programs and is seeking to expand its links with private employers in its next stages.
Source: www.youthbuild.org

Migration Support Programs (Type 2)

Migration for work characterizes most developing economies. In today's more mobile age, migration is both increasing and diversifying – more south-south migration between neighboring countries, and more diverse rural to rural to urban within a nation, as well as the traditional developing to developed country migration. Table 1.1 provided data on the varying weight emigration and immigration plays in individual developing economies, with the three biggest external corridors being Mexico to the United States, former Soviet countries and Ukraine to Russia, and Bangladesh to India.[13] Migrants comprise the vast *majority* of the labor force of key high-income Arabian Peninsula nations (Qatar 87%, United Arab Emirates 70%, Kuwait 69%)[14] creating very different challenges of integration and mobility, particularly for low-skilled migrants from East Asia and the Philippines.

In many of the largest migrating nations, such as the Philippines, programs and institutions have grown up separately from smaller domestic economy-related employment or labor intermediation services, but not always. As Stage 2 evolves, creating, supporting or coordinating with migration programs should mirror the importance of migration as a factor in employment. Services and strategies differ according to whether the objective is facilitating/supporting internal migration, external migration (temporary and curricular), return migration, or migrants working within a country's borders. Reviewing such migration support services by type:

First, supporting *internal migration* or labor mobility within a nation's borders is a principal function of national labor intermediation services. In some developing countries, however, mobility is constrained not only by lack of information but also by loss of eligibility to other services, lack of housing alternatives and by cultural norms, should a person move for work. The starting point is to insure workers know what available jobs there are. This means permitting access to labor market information and job registers whether online or in regional offices, so that labor market information services and job registries have a national reach and national access. Where there are large numbers of unfilled vacancies in particular growing regions, services of specialized recruitment, relocation assistance or job fairs where the unemployed live have been used to move from information to placement. In Poland, where its citizens migrate in large numbers within Europe and Russia, citizens still do not have access to job registries and labor market information to look first in other areas of their own country. Lack of information and open access to vacancies is not typically the only barrier to internal migration, but is often one of the easier and first barriers to address. Internal labor mobility is comparatively low by international standards in developing countries in Central Asia and Eastern Europe.[15] Greater internal labor mobility is a driver worldwide of greater productivity, and, a recent World Bank study argues that, for Europe and Central Asia in particular, both employment and productivity gains could be made through greater internal mobility. Authors Arias and Sanchez-Páramo argue that labor market information would need to be combined with support for housing/credit markets, removal of administrative barriers, and reduction of regional disparities in social services, among other policy changes to improve labor mobility.[16] In the case of Ukraine, a survey indicates that lack of labor market information was cited by 25% of respondents as a barrier to internal mobility, but the official registration system which requires registration of new residencies (a rare administrative requirement worldwide) topped the barriers cited by nearly 40% of respondents inhibiting internal migration.[17]

Second, *emigration* or *external migration* can be made safer, more circular and more human capital-enhancing through listings of authorized foreign employment or seasonal/fixed term migration programs, either run by or coordinated with a labor intermediation service. In the case of programs run directly by labor intermediation services, the comparative advantage is not permanent migration, but rather facilitating and supporting temporary, seasonal and curricular migration, linking it back to the local economy. Turkey's public employment service lists employment abroad as part of its national job bank.[18] The National Employment Services of Guatemala and Mexico manage seasonal agricultural workers and, more recently, temporary services (tourism) workers in the United States. Services to support temporary migration programs include: procurement of visas, oversight and accountability on their return, and off-season training in their home countries. While exploitation unfortunately still occurs as workers fear that reporting abuse would lead to their not returning the next year, these workers have the advantage of being authorized migrants with access to their national consulates, safe border passage, and regulated working conditions. Migration support programs need not be run by a national employment or labor intermediation service, but the goal is linkage to a national job registry to be able to refer workers with the right profile to these programs. This is particularly important to support rural employment. Colombia runs a temporary agricultural workers' program with Spain through its National Training Institute (SENA, *Servicio Nacional de Aprendizaje*) which includes training in Spain and back in Colombia in the off-season when workers return, with the idea of upgrading agricultural skills over time. These programs are all admittedly small, with negotiated numbers of migrants regulated by bilateral agreements. For this reason they are most applicable for seasonal or curricular jobs.

A special case for authorized migration abroad is the use of private placement agencies which bring low-skilled workers – maids, construction workers, services – to the Middle East. Regulation of private recruitment agencies which charge high fees to poor migrants to work under poor, exploitative conditions has proved both inadequate and difficult to enforce as firms quickly move underground to avoid regulation, as found by Philippine migration expert, Dovelyn Rannweig Agunias. These agencies work directly with employers, often bypassing oversight. They recruit individually, not through intermediation services. There is little consensus between origin and destination countries on the management of such firms. Agunias proposes a series of reforms, noting the dilemma that "temporary migration to the region [Middle East] at the current scale would be impossible without private agencies."[19]

A third type of migration more directly supported by labor intermediation services is return migration – reintegrating national migrants back into an economy. Return migration often should not require a specialized program if the labor intermediation service has evolved enough to manage individual cases and is national in scope. By using case management, an employer/counselor can assess the special skills of the return migrant – foreign languages, technical skills (from construction to computers) – for appropriate placement and coordination with any available social services. The small Pacific island nation of Tonga has been cited as an example of a country which used its return migration support programs for returning migrants from New Zealand in an effective way to contribute to national job growth.[20]

A fourth (and final!) migration category is permitting migrants to access labor market services in the country where they are working or looking for work. This is admittedly done less frequently and, when done, has typically covered migrants only from countries under special agreements, such as within the European Union or, in Latin America, through bilateral or regional agreements such as *Mercosur*.[21] Doing this can and has played a role in helping integrate migrants, enabling access to human capital improvements and fueling economic growth. Ireland's public employment service played a particular role in screening and placing Eastern European immigrants (from Poland and Estonia), meeting growing demand fueling Ireland's boom in the 1990s. Argentina, under the framework of Mercosur, bilateral agreements, and a national initiative to provide documents to migrants working in the country, permits Mercosur members access to its public employment service and training programs, particularly relevant for agricultural migrant workers coming typically from neighboring Bolivia and Paraguay.[22]

Microenterprise/Entrepreneurship (Type 2)

Self-employment through microbusinesses is a reality in the developing world, and is the predominant form of employment in many low-income, rural economies such as Laos or Nepal. Entrepreneurship refers to the set of innovation and management skills to create businesses and, hopefully, enable them to grow. The reality of much self-employment for the poor in the developing world is that it enables only survival with limited income growth. How to support viable micro and small businesses is thus a highly relevant policy question across all developing country income levels.

Sound macroeconomic conditions and a good business environment, including roads, regulations and good laws, are needed to enable entrepreneurship to lead to sustainable businesses, and thus to jobs. Entrepreneurship or microenterprise programs are intended to help reduce constraints and enhance the productivity and skills of small-scale entrepreneurs along with the right combination of national conditions. A diverse range of microenterprise programs can be found in developing economies of all income levels, with different emphases on any of a range of labor market factors needed to help make a business viable: credit, management skills, marketing, technical skills. Evaluation studies have been limited and conclusions are not consistent about what is effective for whom and in what contexts. We do know that available credit is a dominant constraint, and that entrepreneurial skills and traits are strongly related to the success of a business. Cho and Honorati conducted a meta regression analysis of 37 impact evaluations, not all of which explicitly concerned self-employment programs.[23] They did reach some interesting conclusions. They found that a package of support promoting skills and financing support had larger labor market impacts and that vocational and business training worked better than financial training. There were big differences in gender, with the largest effects overall coming from providing women with access to credit.[24] What has been learned is how tailored to local market needs and norms is enterprise development. Labor intermediation services have their roots and design in formal labor markets; they may not have the specialized personnel and access to all the tools to be the best provider of this type of employment support program. A study of the institutional delivery of entrepreneurship for women in rural India found different results and different service needs as a result of different social norms for women, according to whether they were upper or lower caste Hindu women or Muslim women, even within the same village.[25]

Public employment services in developing countries or their public-private variants differ as to whether they have microenterprise training as a service menu option, but few are able to offer the full range of non-labor services needed to make such microenterprises viable – credit, technical advice, and marketing. Entrepreneurship programs particularly for young people are routinely offered in the Middle East and North Africa, but rarely, according to the World Bank, by public employment services.[26] Latin American public employment services often have microenterprise training as a menu option but typically these are one-shot training courses without the wider set of complementary services of credit, marketing and supervision. Some Ministry of Labor programs are tasked with approving individual business plans and small credits (such as for carpentry supplies), but by staff with often no training or business experience or mandate to follow the business over years.

Public-private labor intermediation services need to look very closely at the range of needs and national experience for viable microentrepreneurship; and, from that, what provider(s) and services package are the best option for that country context. India has pioneered the self-help model for microenterprise development in rural areas. Self-help groups have then been connected with first informal and later formal credit institutions. Particularly when self-employment is the only local employment option, only these adapted models have the ability to identify local constraints, be they social, infrastructure, or market-related. An impact evaluation of rural delivery mechanisms for microenterprise training in rural Indian self-help groups reached very context-specific conclusions.[27] It found that training increased assets but not income. It found that underlying conditions that enabled female microentrepreneurs to benefit from training were good (paved) village roads and the linkage model chosen, specifically banks providing loans and NGOs the organization, or banks financing NGOs to provide loans.[28] Use of government training organizers had poorer results. A labor intermediation services role in rural, self-employment-dominated economies would mostly likely only be relevant as an information base and for those seeking urban employment. In analyzing private versus public sector delivery of entrepreneurship programs, Cho and Honorati found better performance over the long term from the private sector.[29] This is particularly useful in providing business counseling and market contacts. As these programs are already offered by a range of NGO, private and public providers, labor intermediation services should consider their value-added as a referral service if they do not have the experienced personnel or ability to deliver the range of services needed to make such programs viable.

Placement/Human Resources Services for Employers (Type 2)

A final type of service that plays an enhanced role in intermediation is when a labor intermediation service does directly the work of a human resource department of a private firm. This can include testing, screening, writing job descriptions, interviewing potential candidates, and then sending the selected candidates to the firm for final review. While most public employment services are not allowed to charge fees to job seekers, they can charge employers for services and I have seen these services both bring in needed cash and help increase placement. Only large firms typically have the resources for formal human resources departments, and in developing countries, with micro, small and medium-sized business constituting the vast majority of employment, such a service contributes to both firm and worker productivity through a better quality match and reduced time to search for and hire employees. In these cases, the public-private intermediation service can pre-select candidates from the national register, assess their readiness and refer only the candidates who best fit. Particularly in countries with little experience of open job registers, firms may first fear an onslaught of candidates from open listings. Over time, as even small firms learn how to define the parameters of what they are looking for in potential employees, those who receive specialized placement services may migrate to open registry as is the case in Jamaica.

Type 3: Program Administration and Support Services Referral

Before exhausting you further, a final type of service in Stage 2 is administration or referral to other labor market and social programs. The most typical program and, in fact, the origin of employment services in advanced countries, involved also administering unemployment insurance. Program administration is not a service to directly aid better job placement, like "intermediation plus" services described under Type 2, but rather to provide a similar client with more coordinated program supports that go together with job hunting. More and more advanced and developing countries are moving to co-locate and coordinate a range of social and labor market services in "one stop" shops. This more modern for is an important management and policy reforms discussed in the next section and in Chap. 5. In this section, we lay out what it entails when the labor intermediation services, often the same counselors who refer job seekers to jobs and work on job hunting strategies, are also in charge of administering other labor market or social programs or referring job seekers to other services.

Many, if not most, of the advanced countries started their public employment services also administering unemployment insurance (UI) or other labor market program supports. This was done for good conceptual reasons: if unemployment insurance is to be provided under the condition that the recipient uses the income support to spend time looking for a good job, then an employment service counselor can both support and check up on whether the recipient is actually looking for a job. One can understand that having a job search service in the same place where you pick up your unemployment insurance check was designed to help insure that those getting the checks were actually looking for work. Interestingly, over time, some countries – like the United States, for instance – completely separated the two and now the verification of job search is done online or on the phone (not particularly well, mind you!).

Unemployment insurance is far less prevalent in developing countries, whether low- or middle-income. More developing economies started job search assistance services (Stage 1) without having cash incentives to get job seekers through the door. Even in developing countries that have a form of unemployment insurance or unemployment assistance (UA), it is far less likely that it is delivered in the same place as job search assistance. Argentina and the Bahamas are examples[30] of separate administration; in Turkey, UI is administered through the public employment service. This is more a function of which ministry owned which program, limited fiscal resources, and the relative weakness of job search services in developing countries, as well as the technical difficulties of verifying job search in highly informal economies. Brazil, for instance, which has a relatively short-term unemployment insurance program, is now trying to link its employment service with its unemployment insurance program.

Labor Market Program Administration/Unemployment Support (Type 3)

Given that labor market or social programs are publically financed, they are run in developing countries by the corresponding domestic agency, often a social or labor ministry. With great variety by region in the developing world, public employment services – whether on the road to creating labor intermediation services with private or NGO partners or not – may have started with the responsibility for also administering other labor market or social programs. Many Eastern European, Middle Eastern, and North African systems started public employment services with other program administration, even if it wasn't unemployment insurance in name.

Starting a service from the beginning with the responsibilities of program administration only partially related to job search typically makes it more difficult for developing countries with limited resources and personnel to prioritize effective private sector job search among its management responsibilities.

In program administration, the key for labor intermediation services in developing countries is the impact on the responsibilities/workload for job counselors, the training received to administer programs, and the alignment of incentives within various programs to an employment mission. Switzerland's job counselors must explicitly verify where the UI recipient is looking for work, and then – and this is rare – they have the authority to dock a portion of a UI recipient's payment if they are not actively looking for work. While this is a linkage only the most formal and advanced labor markets can do effectively, developing countries must still be concerned with the balance between supporting workers' incomes while unemployed and assisting those same individuals to be reemployed and job placement. In a survey of 73 public employment services covering both developed and developing countries, only the regions of Europe and Asia-Pacific strongly reported the incorporation of unemployment insurance and passive policies for the unemployed[31]; such policies were much rarer in Africa and the Americas. Mexico's national employment service ran a UI-type income support program of two separate payments for those laid off from the formal sector. With no explicit linkage to looking for work, overloaded job counselors across Mexico basically used their limited time with clients to verify their unemployment status and start the paperwork for the program. The answer is not to have separate program administrators meet with the same clients unless the programs do not affect incentives and quality of job search, such as with social assistance.

As Stage 2 progresses, job counselors should have a range of program tools in their tool box, but care is required to insure that job counselors have the ability to assign programs to the individuals who need them most. More often than not, in developing countries, program administrators are in charge of who is enrolled in their programs; job counselors don't have much ability to refer or enroll job seekers in other labor market or social programs. Empowering job counselors with the administrative ability to utilize and tailor different programs for different client needs lies at the heart of case management, discussed in the next section.

Social Service Gateway and Referral (Type 3)

While once more the purview of advanced countries, increasingly middle-income countries may offer access to social services or referral to social services within a labor intermediation service as a way of better coordinating effective social and labor market interventions for the poor. Turkey's public employment service ISKUR expanded greatly after 2008, and now links all recipients of social services to ISKUR's employment database and services.[32] Social services in much poorer countries have a very different program history from those in the advanced countries where, over time, labor market connections have been infused in as conditions to anti-poverty programs in various "welfare-to-work" schemes, most notably in the United States and the United Kingdom. Conditional and unconditional cash transfer programs (CTs and CCTs) – innovative income support for the poor now widely diffused in the developing world – have universally sprung up across all regions based on the first, and rigorously tested, models in Brazil and Mexico. These CCT and CT social assistance programs for the poor from their beginnings have been run separate from labor market programs and policies and are almost universally wider in coverage. Having started as different programs, a number of higher-income developing countries, such as Chile and Brazil, are now looking to better integrate labor market programs into their current social policy framework. These new innovations are discussed in Chapter 5 where a number of future models are discussed in greater detail.

To conclude this section, new and linked services are not ends in themselves but are tools contributing to the second big-picture change of the next section – expanding performance, coverage and impact of what is now a labor intermediation service. To have such effects, extended services need to be introduced sequentially, focusing on the most needed services for underserved populations (new youth entrants for example). The sequencing must give attention to who and how to administer the new service, so as not to overwhelm nascent administrative capacity or create perverse incentives, together with which services are performing well in a given economy. I have seen services fragment too early into too many services serving too few people. In the Middle East and North Africa region, World Bank specialists found many national employment services providing a variety of programs but the impact and cost-effectiveness of individual programs have not been assessed.[33] That is why in Stage 2 expansion of services must move in combination with management reforms and better monitoring and evaluation.

Which service to sequence when? Done strategically, either "intermediation plus" services (Type 2) *or* labor/social program administration/support (Type 3) would typically be used early on in "job-poor" environments to serve clients who could not easily get employment via open vacancies. A basic form of information service (Type 1) should be considered an early base service as Stage 2 begins, with middle- and high-income countries likely having more national capacity to begin with a more comprehensive databank. Beyond these extended services, sequencing in migration or microenterprise and other program administration reflects labor markets as distinct as the countries themselves.

BUILDING A BETTER SERVICE: ADVANCING COVERAGE AND EFFICIENCY THROUGH MANAGEMENT RESTRUCTURING, CASE MANAGEMENT, MONITORING AND EVALUATION

As the employment services platform is expanded progressively through new and linked services into labor intermediation services it will confront an inevitable management challenge. Moving from a base of core employment services with a few extended information and program services will require a more streamlined and professionalized management, staff upgrading, and better monitoring and evaluation so that one can know what intermediation services are working well for whom. Much of the more recent innovation in the advanced countries has happened through such management rethinking and restructuring.

This section looks at the key elements of expanding coverage and improving performance of what can now be called labor intermediation services. First it looks broadly at management restructuring for expansion and better performance. This restructuring has two principal higher level forms: (1) case management – the technique to focus strategies and tailor services to individual employment needs; and, (2) "one stop" service consolidation – combining services in the same location, termed "one stop" services. The section concludes with the important focus on monitoring and evaluation which lies at the heart of understanding how this new labor intermediation service is meeting client needs. More than in other parts of the book, lessons from the advanced countries from Australia to Great Britain are instructive, particularly for the middle-income developing countries.

Management Platform for Expansion and Better Performance

Without intense focus on improving management, developing country labor intermediation services with or without supporting private sector partners are often constrained in expanding service provision with job seekers discouraged by inefficient processes, long waits, and a mismatch between what they need to get a job and what the employment service has to offer. Before even considering moving to higher order management restructuring, such as that involved in case management or one stop shops, developing countries should give an intense second look at two management dimensions needed for expansion with better performance: (1) central/local office autonomy and distribution; and, (2) organization of the workflow and ability to attend to clients.

On balancing central versus decentralized management, a growing labor intermediation service may either be building from essentially a core service in the capital or principal cities outward, or may already be a network of public with private employment offices. Herein often lies a bureaucratic struggle between standardizing processes and office organization at the national level and permitting greater flexibility to adapt to local employers and job seekers at the local level (always the go-to preference when it comes to matching labor supply and demand). Chile decentralized to local municipal centers all employment program and job placement services; Costa Rica essentially started its intermediation services from a decentralized platform, making greater use of online services. Tunisia's public employment service has developed over time a wide assortment of very different centers, some oriented to specific sectors. Local flexibility in the management of clients and relationships with local employers is key; national functions should emphasize the quality of a national system/labor market, standard setting, and technical support. The public employment services of Benin, Vietnam, the Dominican Republic, Paraguay and Uruguay reported their systems as having high levels of local flexibility in five of six different dimensions, the highest being local flexibility in management and local development networks and the least in the design of policies and programs.[34]

The computer management system that handled core employment functions and perhaps one or two other services in Stage 1 will need an overall technical review and possible redesign if it is to handle more clients more efficiently with more instruments in Stage 2. Are there the equipment, internal procedures, and training of staff that can provide a platform for expansion? How can information-intake processes be streamlined? Do job counselors have time to attend to the clients with the greatest needs?

Reorganizing workflows and upgrading computer and information systems (with training) should be done with an eye to moving eventually to case management. I have seen developing country services talk case management before they had an information system that could register clients and what services they were receiving!

There are a number of critical elements of a more efficient management structure, drawing lessons again from both OECD and middle-income developing country services:

- A database and information system capable of recording client job-relevant information, and ultimately (for case management) recording services received, job search strategy and follow-up;
- A simplified intake system for registering clients and companies in this database, done by self-service or receptionist/assistants;
- Facilities for self-service registration, self-service use of computers, call-in telephone services and online, as relevant to the local population. In addition to online services, developing countries are using kiosks in shopping malls or cell phone notices accessible to those without computers;
- "Workflow" reorganization to balance staffing, skills, and work demands, importantly so that clients are immediately attended to and basic information is inputted by administrators if not by the job seekers themselves;
- Organization of job counselor functions with training, potentially permitting counselors to specialize in certain types of occupation, and to register both vacancies and job seekers.

This work reorganization and modernization can operate on two levels: national and local walk-in office levels. The state of San Luis Potosí in North-Central Mexico restructured its own workflow, the work of job counselors versus receptionists versus private sector job promoters, and set office goals, still delivering within the program requirements of the national employment service which did not go through the same process.[35]

The internet offers greater potential to offer services and attend to clients online, as long as it is commensurate and proportional to access and use in the country. Graph 4.1 displays the growth rates in internet usage by developing country income category: an upward trajectory for all nations, but at much lower levels for lower levels of national income.

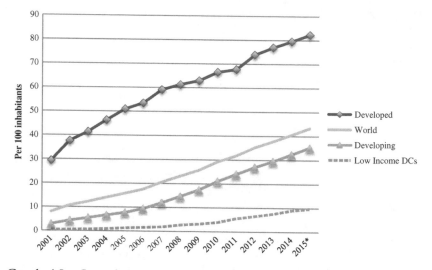

Graph 4.1   Growth in individuals using the internet by country income classification
(Source: *ITU World Telecommunication/ICT Indicators*, 2015. Figures for 2001–2015 are estimated. Country classifications are based on UN M49, see: http://www.itu.int/en/ITU-D/Statistics/Pages/definitions/regions.aspx.html)

Case Management and Professionalization of Job Counselors

"Case management" – where well-trained counselors are assigned a set of job seekers/clients to support and advise through multiple services – is becoming the norm within the advanced nations but is much rarer in the developing world. One can see how, with so many factors needed to work together for someone to get, keep, and grow in a job, focusing on individual cases would help those who need it get the right complement of services, while those who don't need it would not be channeled into unnecessary and costly other interventions.

Case management is not new. Some trace it back to the early settler movement in the United States. It was more universally applied first in health care, but more consistently to employment promotion beginning in Sweden in 1935, New Zealand in 1995 and the United Kingdom in 1997.[36] Case management for employment typically encompasses a diagnosis of needs/skills, individualized job search assistance and strategy, coordination with complementary training or education, and career development. Case management requires going well beyond placement (the objective of basic employment services) to a complementary range of employment-related services, the heart of Stage 2 for labor intermediation services.

Quite a number of things need to be in place before moving to case management delivery: a good information system, counselors trained and knowledgeable about the services and local employment, and, not minor in developing countries, a set of tools/programs that can be employed to offer a client. In terms of sequencing, tools for diagnosing worker/job seeker needs should not come before either the information system or the ability to assign/refer workers to programs. Sounds logical, but mostly I have seen it the other way! Countries buy off-the-shelf diagnostic tools or testing, and yet have not worked out how or even whether the information can be put to good use and whether counselors have the ability to keep track of the case. This is one of many examples in this book when borrowing off-the-shelf developed country techniques can be misapplied or sequenced too early, undermining the goal of improved outcomes.

A number of middle- to high-income developing countries have advanced to employing case management in the delivery of social services. Future developing country models may be able to join case management in labor intermediation services through a social service door, as examined in Chapter 5 which looks to the near future. Lower-income developing countries will not likely have the resources or set of programs to evolve to an extensive case management system, but there is no doubt that *current* service provision could be reorganized to permit more clients to be served better with the same level of resources – that is, employing the principles of case management to improve outcomes and performance.

A first principle of case management relevant to employment search is the apportionment of services based on individual need. A common perverse incentive in developing countries is that more expensive services, such as training or microenterprise support, may be apportioned to those who don't need them to get a job or the training/microenterprise support does not fit the individual's profile or the market's need and is, in fact, a wasted service. One way to begin to address this is by tighter eligibility criteria. A second is to permit the job counselor to assign/refer job seekers to programs based on an assessment of whether they can benefit. This is often not done in countries where different ministries (and sometimes different political parties) control discrete employment-related programs. Even in the same intermediation service office, in the same ministry, you can have different individuals responsible for filling only the rosters of their respective programs, creaming off either the best candidates or just the ones who walk through the door. In such cases, permitting more open registration of programs on which trained job counselors could register applicants would be a step forward in efficiency and tailoring program use to its utility for the individual.

A second case management principle to apply, even before and while case management is being adopted, is upgrading the role of a job counselor. This includes reducing administrative burdens, upgrading job tasks, and improving their training and qualifications. The job counselor registers both jobs and job seekers and advises on job search and training; knowledge of local employment and human resource development is needed to do the job well. In a fair number of labor intermediation services, there can be a separate specialized role working just with the private sector to unearth and register jobs, termed a job broker or private sector counselor. Inputting profile data is still often done by overworked job counselors in developing countries but, for the many job seekers who cannot access computers, this job can be devolved to a receptionist or a technical assistant overseeing self-registration on a bank of computers or to a telephone receptionist. In addition, increasing self-services, or other quicker services for less complicated cases, such as telephone inquiries and online services, is important, so that, over time, the job counselor is able to concentrate more person-to-person services on the more difficult-to-employ. A 2014 survey of public employment services worldwide found substantial regional variation in the use of quicker access services: online services were used extensively in Asia and the Pacific region, including China and Singapore (over 90%) in comparison to Africa (15%), telephone call centers were much less widely used in Asia (62%), and used in over 45% of the 13 African services surveyed.[37] There is still much room for systematizing the core employment service instruments in most developing economies as a necessary step to move progressively to case management. Even for developing countries well into Stage 2, job counselors still routinely meet with clients only to enter their basic profile data and match them to a public or private job register.

As job tasks and management systems are upgraded, the management overhaul must be accompanied with a similar zest for training and career development for job counselors and other professionals of an intermediation service. This includes both specific training for the use of information systems and programs managed by the service, as well as seminars to improve staff knowledge of the local labor market. As the job counselor is able to concentrate more and more on serving individuals, this is when analytical tools can be phased in as relevant to the pool seeking employment.

Thus a sequence of improved management processes and staff upgrading lays the foundation for a case management system. Only through case management can providers (public or private) develop and effectively monitor the job search plan of an individual job seeker. Estonia now manages individual job search plans within a comprehensive case management system linking social benefits, unemployment insurance and labor intermediation.[38]

Systematic evidence on the improvements brought about by case management comes largely from developed country systems which have had years of implementation experience. US experimental welfare-to-work evaluations have investigated the differential impacts of traditional case management, where income support and employment assistance were given separately, and integrated case management, where both functions were brought together. The results found that integrated case managers provided more personalized attention, engaged more people in welfare-to-work activities, and more closely monitored participation in program activities. Both approaches reduced welfare receipt and payments, but the effects of the integrated program were somewhat larger.[39] In a subsequent analysis, summarizing findings from experimental studies on service strategies in 59 different employment offices across the USA, researchers reported higher employment and earnings impacts in those offices where case managers delivered a personalized service and placed an emphasis on quick job entry.[40] A study of Denmark found also that intensive job search assistance and frequent caseworker meetings were highly cost-effective in shortening spells of unemployment.[41] A case management approach – or even employing case management principles – is aided by the consolidated delivery of services from one office, named for the US variant "the one stop shop."

Single Window and Co-location

As intermediation services expand both in the number of clients and the range of products available, effectiveness will center on their ability to deliver what seems to be a contradiction – more services to more people in an easier and more streamlined fashion. In a world of too many stops for too many services, labor intermediation services are combining to create service "centers" to both entice more clients through the door and create better links with services people need to support themselves and their families. Many OECD systems and localities have placed the job exchange function within a "one stop shop" concept – where a range of employment-related programs and often social services can be accessed in the same place (both virtual and physical). One stop shops in OECD countries have expanded well beyond labor market programs to include registration of new businesses, support to microenterprises, health services, and child care, for example.

The simplest first form, used often in the United States, is simply "co-location" – having available services in the same physical location. This is actually a model to consider for many developing countries. In the United States, co-location has its advantages with so many different national, state and local programs. In developing countries, it is often not easy to slay the bureaucratic dragons in the way of inducing diverse ministries to register and deliver services together; a first step could be getting these distinct ministries to see the advantages of co-habiting! Transportation costs are also a factor for the poor to access services; locating services together aids both ease of delivery and greater information on the range of services altogether. Co-location is particularly useful when applied to microenterprise services, as it often requires coordination of services outside the purview and expertise of either labor or social ministries. In a One Stop Shop in Northern Virginia, USA, a small business assistance center was located on a different floor. Employment counselors on the floor below merely referred those interested in self-employment to the center which had state and private financing and offered specialized business counselors, information on bank loans and credits, and technical assistance for micro and small businesses.[42]

A second form for developing countries in Stage 2 would be housing existing active policies (training and intermediation) and passive, unemployment insurance (if available) in a "single window." The single window is a major step-up as it means one common registration form, and one central information window to learn about access to programs. In this way, job seekers can access in the same place information on job openings, training, and labor market trends, and access to their unemployment insurance or other employment protection programs. By consolidating registration and access, services can be better tailored to the needs of the individual (via case management) and bureaucratic inefficiencies can be reduced, so that the intermediation function is accomplished faster and with better outcomes for job seekers. Social programs increasingly link with labor market programs in single window reforms in developing countries. Peru, for example, has transitioned all its labor market programs under its *ventanilla única* (single window in Spanish).

The United Kingdom called its consolidation "One," terming it a "single work-focused gateway" bringing together employment services, the social benefits authority, and local government programs. The UK tested different models of the "One" service – a basic model, a call center variant, and a version delivered by private and NGO providers, finding that one model even of a one stop shop might not fit all regions.

Improving Monitoring and Evaluation

Developing effective monitoring of labor intermediation services and evaluating both the service and the distinct programs supported by the service are an essential feature of Stage 2. In Eastern and Central Europe, for example, public employment services grew up with a social assistance mindset, a right for all beneficiaries, rather than the right to effective interventions. It is often a mindset change to a culture of accountability. The use of a range of monitoring indicators regarding the quality of job obtained, such as job retention, wages and benefits, and earnings gains has been found to make it less likely that either public or private providers will place participants in poor quality jobs.[43]

Continual refinement of intermediation instruments, programs and services is the only way to keep services relevant to a changing economy and workforce. Research has continued to show that impacts for active labor market policies can be quite modest to zero, but design is the key. And you can't tell if the design fits a developing country labor market without your own monitoring and evaluation.

Impact evaluations are particularly needed to advance in Stage 2. To date, they have been used more often to assess the impact of training programs. But a meta-analysis review found that developing country positive impacts (short-term) for employment services were relatively consistent with the results for developed countries.[44] In one of the few recent impact evaluations of a developing country employment service, the Inter-American Development Bank found that the job placement and income earnings were positive for men versus a control group, but not significant for women. Only with this kind of information can the Mexican National Employment Service redouble its efforts and increase monitoring to ensure that women's employment prospects are improved.

As services move to intermediate on a variety of fronts, impact evaluations just measuring job placement results will be insufficient. Testing whether it was one specific intervention that got the job versus a similar person who didn't use that one intervention is tricky. First, research shows that the multiple methods for job search should be used to find work. Someone might have gotten a job through an intermediation service but it is not recorded anywhere; they might have gotten the information about a job from an intermediation service's job fair or announcement, but they record in a survey they got their job on their own. Second, one of the important and different roles needed to be played by labor intermediation services in developing countries is to help the external market work better (see next section). That is, a national public-private service is also seeking to stimulate more self-service and combined methods, so it is playing a secondary or indirect role in more job placements. For this reason, impact evaluations combined with other monitoring and evaluation instruments will provide a bigger picture. The following summarizes the key information bases, and monitoring and evaluation instruments particularly relevant to Stage 2.

Monitoring instruments also play a greater management role in Stage 2, to help monitor the effectiveness of discrete offices and discrete interventions. South Korea founded an Employment Services Evaluation Center in 2006 as part of its set of information services. In 2009, they simplified into one composite monitoring index for offices which combines placement rates, customer satisfaction, and duration with employer. A single performance evaluation index weights job placement together with the difficulty of placement measured by the local employment rate.[45] Other performance management systems in the advanced countries that use regression models on the role of local labor market conditions include Switzerland, Germany and Australia. Mexico has developed a performance monitoring system of over 60 indicators and annually pits its regional offices in an annual competition for "top state employment service" which has both motivated and rewarded higher levels of service within the system. The Swiss system, for example, measures all its state ("canton") offices against four principal criteria, but places particular weight on the speed of getting workers into new jobs, whereas the British system, with more entrenched long-term unemployment, places more weight on the ability to retain the worker in a new job over a longer period.

Experience from advanced, middle-income and developing countries demonstrates that all systems are refining and adapting their performance measures, incentives and instruments to changing economies and markets. Performance indicators are particularly important when services strive to improve the quality of the job match for job seekers. Past research has indicated that inclusion of indicators such as those related to job retention, wages and benefits, earnings gains, all help diminish any incentive to place participants in poor quality jobs in both public and private providers.[46]

Performance-based contracting, including the elements of paying for employment outcomes, was first developed in the United States and subsequently extended to the UK, Australia and the Netherlands.[47] Other countries have recently implemented or are testing changes in their employment services contracts with several, such as Germany, France, Denmark, Sweden, and Israel, experimenting with job outcome performance contracts and delivery through for-profit providers.

The United Kingdom originally benchmarked public against private providers and evolved to its current "pay for performance" system which pays more for longer job insertion. Latin American systems have begun making strides in management reforms and innovations via the use of "quality control" systems, these can include measuring customer satisfaction, efficiency of service, and quality of placement which are certified to international (ISO 9000) standards. San Luis Potosí, one of the state systems in the Mexican National Employment Service, has been recognized for its best practice in such systems (Kappaz and Rosa 2009).

Stage 2: *Monitoring and Data Collection*

- Comprehensive beneficiary databases which record and track clients of the service, including among the following indicators: instances of service delivery (e.g. date of visits to walk-in centers), the type of service delivered and record of completion, employment (e.g. initiation date, salary). For those using case management, the individual (case) plan is recorded including the schedule of agreed services, follow-up visits to the intermediation center, and employment retention over defined periods (e.g. six-month intervals), and accomplishment of the plan.
- Comprehensive data collected on beneficiary characteristics supporting as well impact evaluations (e.g. age, sex, employment history) either in select regions or nationally, potentially including race, disability and indigenous origin.

- Administrative and performance input data, including spending (on personnel, programs, compliance), staff hours, staff-to-clients-served ratios.
- Labor market indicators measured typically via a labor observatory and labor force surveys, including unemployment rates by sector, age, salaries, benefits.

Stage 2: *Performance, Output and Impact Indicators*

- Impact: rate of labor market insertion, disaggregated by gender, ethnic group/indigenous peoples (if data permits).
- Outputs: vacancy fill rate, individual plans completed, referrals (e.g. to training, counseling, social services).
- Performance: rate and increasing rate of labor market insertion; increase in job listings and placements at higher income levels; comparative performance of regional offices.
- Cost-efficiency: cost per worker who finds employment, unit costs for extended programs and services, cost of training versus other programs for similar outcomes.

Stage 2: *Evaluation Types and Instruments*

- Impact evaluations, experimental and quasi-experimental on both specific training programs managed by the intermediation service and the intermediation service itself. More advanced systems may be able to combine impact plus cost of intervention (versus alternatives).
- Cost-benefit analysis[48] of specific services as well as of the intermediation service overall (e.g. cost per worker inserted in new employment, benefit savings with unemployment insurance, social assistance).
- Process evaluations examining the efficiency of delivery of service.
- Client and employer satisfaction surveys.

TOWARDS A NATIONAL INTERMEDIATION "SYSTEM": CREATING JOBS INC.

Finally, the third "big-picture" change for developing countries in Stage 2 is to view the intermediation function between job seekers, jobs, training and education as a "market" of public, private, and non-profit providers in which independent job search is facilitated as much as possible and more intermediation happens via improved market forces. By moving the policy lens from making a service work better to making the wider market work better as well will make wider impacts possible. In this intermediation market, some will be principally intermediation agents – public employment services, private placement agencies, and electronic services – but most, and hopefully, more and more, intermediation would be "embedded" in the programs of a wider range of actors and providers in which job placement is part of the outcomes. Making this market work better as an inter connected intermediation system can have wider market effects: inducing schools and training institutions to be more accountable for getting graduates good jobs; getting firms to promote more learning in the workplace for both employees and trainees; creating incentives for training and hiring to be done more by commonly accepted standards so the young and old are able to plan careers by developing their human capital.

Thinking about intermediation as a "market system" of different public, private and non-profit means changing traditional ideas that other intermediation actors are always direct competitors for the same set of clients – your market gain is my market loss. This is particularly true for developing country public employment services that would need to devote scarce funds to expanding the market for non-public providers and perhaps not getting all the political glory that goes along with it. Case after developing country case in this book, however, has shown the opposite to be true. With a lens focused on widening the market outside the public sector, not only does the small public employment service pie get bigger, but many more varieties of pies are made in the process. The public sector cook can still get political compliments without doing all the baking!

It is worth remembering our labor market's modesty here. Active labor market policies – as they are currently conceptualized – work independently and have modest effects, at best. Classic public employment services – even the largest ones – have limited market coverage, at best. If the new jobs agenda is economic growth through good, and more productive, job creation then national labor intermediation services in developing countries need to think as well about their role in aiding a better functioning intermediation system with the idea of coaxing the national labor market out of some of its key market failures: poor information; lack of labor transparency; uncompetitive hiring. This cannot be done by more services alone, but rather how these services and coordinating policy actions induce the labor market into greater numbers of open job listings, more competition or merit-based hiring; less time, more efficient, and more productive job searches. The effects on jobs would be most important on the areas of an economy that are growing (if there are) and that is why this section ends and the next chapter begins with intermediation and targeting growing sectors.

This final "big picture" section of Stage 2 first takes a quick snapshot look at these varied public-private-NGO models of national intermediation services which would be the principal drivers and supporters of stimulating a more interconnected national system improving intermediation. The section then looks at some specific policy lines to help promote a more interconnected intermediation "system" that *both* enlarges who intermediates and how they do it more efficiently to contribute to employment. It ends with applying the national intermediation market system lens first to growing economic sectors.

Varied Models of National Intermediation Services in Even More Varied National Intermediation Markets

By the later stages of Stage 2, developing country labor intermediation services, now national, are very different from the classic national public employment service of old. It is important, though, that Stage 2 is not seen just as the strengthening of a national, formerly all-public, labor intermediation service, but that the service is seen to be playing a different foundational and catalytic role in a national intermediation "system." This rethinking of system impact happens for a formerly solely public employment service on two planes: first, via the continually evolving public-private-NGO administrative configuration and contracting arrangements of the national service; and second, via the services themselves.

First, sub-contracting or shared administrative responsibilities with private and non-profit providers has been the principal mechanism in developed and developing countries for inducing new providers into the marketplace who almost never make their business solely by contracting to the public sector. Research is solid that the use of private contractors with performance monitoring gets better outcomes as well as stimulating a larger market of better intermediaries, via greater competition among more providers.[49] Ingenus, a United Kingdom-based private intermediation services company, grew first through contracts with the public employment service to doing intermediation services internationally. Ingenus now has the contract for the entire Saudi Arabian intermediation system, for example.

Private or non-profit providers have been contracted to run the entire spectrum – from specific services (Turkey), a regional office of a public service (Ceará, Brazil) and a whole service (Saudi Arabia). Moser and Sol argue that many OECD countries have gradually substituted the public employment service for private providers over the last two decades, first for special groups but more recently for the more basic placement functions.[50] By building a set of national intermediation providers over many years, Australia moved to a fully contracted-out public employment service with a sophisticated rating system for providers based on performance.

Australia with perhaps the most evolved set of "star" ratings for all its private providers evolved this ratings system over a decade, learning by doing. The system establishes "pay-for-performance" criteria related to the difficulty of insertion for different types of job seekers, paying for better, quicker and more lasting labor insertion. The results of the "star" system feed back each year and "rate" each of the private providers. The Australian system evolved from one largely focused on improving competition among newly developing providers to a more advanced contracting-out model that rewards providers who get better employment results with higher ratings each year. The Australian Jobs Network has reported dramatic reductions in average costs via the use of its performance -based system. In the Australian case, private providers must accept a package of clients from the easiest to the most difficult to re-employ and are paid based on performance and level of difficulty.[51] The Australian case, among others, demonstrates as well that even the most advanced countries have gone through, and are continuing to go through, years of experimenting and stimulating a private intermediation market to get to their current configuration.

Private and non-profit providers collaborate in many different administrative roles apart from direct contracting. Whether they are service providers without direct contracts (Honduras), collaborators via mutual agreement (Jamaica), or part of local oversight councils (Mexico), these should be seen as channels for market change or expansion. These changes may be indirect but summed together can have market effects, including inducing more firms to openly list vacancies, and improved articulation of private sector employment and skill needs. The models of national intermediation services working with public, private and NGO institutions are in continual development in both the developed and developing world. They span a great range and include:

- Completely privatized national intermediation service (e.g. Australia's Job Network);
- Single private provider of a national employment service (e.g. Saudi Arabia) or private provision of some state services within a national public service (e.g. Brazil)
- Contracted services for the long-term unemployed with reliance on a public employment service for the recently unemployed (up to 12 months) (e.g. United Kingdom);[52]
- Wide-ranging private and NGO market with smaller (comparatively) and highly decentralized public employment service linked with unemployment insurance (e.g. Switzerland).
- Highly decentralized set of municipal employment centers with extensive use of private contracting for training and services (e.g. Chile);
- Reliance principally on private provision with distinct state-level capacities (e.g. the United States);
- Independent public service with Ministry of Labor heading board of directors and NGO provision (e.g. Lebanon);
- Solely public intermediation service with large number of diverse regional offices (e.g. Tunisia).

Market expansion can secondarily be promoted by a multi-pronged national intermediation service by explicitly incorporating other providers in their services. This has been done in developing countries via a national service's electronic platform and linked or integrated job databases, via its job fairs and via promotional events. Mexico's national employment portal, *el Portal de Empleo,* lets private placement companies also list jobs on its national page and participate in their job fairs. If you search for work on a bank of computers in most developing countries, you are typically shown and get access to any job banks. Jamaica's Electronic Labour Exchange (ELE) staff input jobs from newspaper employment ads in order to streamline job search for its users. As these efforts are largely ad hoc to date, it is not clear how much market expansion can be stimulated through consolidation and cooperation in services. However, in the future, this growth can be tracked and efforts made more systematic by including indicators on the growth of the market – for example, number of national listings and placements by source, and number of traineeships using on-the-job methods or contacts with the intermediation service.

Few assessments have been made to map and understand different developing country contexts for intermediation which might also better detect weaknesses and potential directions for contracting or service collaboration. Table 4.2 provides such a mapping exercise for the Middle East. The Middle East demonstrates the great diversity between high reliance on non-governmental providers (e.g. Yemen) to high reliance on the public sector (e.g. Tunisia).

This look at institutional mapping in the Middle East shows how different the fundamentals of national intermediation systems are even in the same region. As described in Box 3.3., Korea built into a system today that connects with its Korea Employment Information Service (KEIS) municipal job centers, special job centers for persons with disabilities (the latter two run by non-profit agencies), 9000 private employment agencies and 2000 temporary help agencies.[53] Market stimulation efforts by less developed economies would need to take on very different dimensions, given the big differences in capacities and scale of market. Particularly in smaller countries, pairing with experienced internal providers has been drawn on more frequently. Institutional strengthening and training in project management for employment are likely needed for many non-governmental organizations, but would be more needed in countries with few organizations, private or NGO working in private sector demand-driven fields. Chile's National Youth Program, *Chile Joven*, was launched through open competitive bidding in a country without many private firms or NGOs who had experience as intermediaries – finding job placement slots for potential trainees in firms and then designing the training. For each periodic bid, they provided training sessions on proposal design and practices to enter this new field of demand-driven training.

In thinking differently about the big picture – a more interconnected national system that promotes better job and skill intermediation – the end goal is not a super-service that can be all things to all job seekers. Rather the question might be to think more strategically about what is needed to create a larger and more and more self-propelling intermediation market, and set targets and programs accordingly. Three other components, or perhaps sub-strategies, of this larger, more interconnected intermediation system include: more employment-accountable schools and training institutions; the encouragement of human resources development as a career and market; and targeting employment growth sectors.

Table 4.2   A snapshot of public-private intermediation markets: Middle East and North Africa, 2010

Country	Registered job seekers		Public sector		Private + NGO sectors	
	Number (thousands)	Percentage of women	Responsible Ministry or Public Employment Agency	# of Regional Offices	# of NGO's Providing Services	# of Private Employment Agencies
Egypt, Arab Republic	895.1	23.3%	Ministry of Manpower and Migration	307	3	54
Jordan	28	–	Department of Employment and Training	14	–	45
Lebanon	12.2ᵃ	–	National Employment Office, MoL	3	4	0
Morocco	517	40.6%	National Agency for Employment and Skills Promotion (ANAPEC)	74	Data not available	Data not available
Syrian Arab Republic	1703.8	31.9%	Central Nomination Unit, Directorate of Labor, Ministry of Social Affairs and Labor (MoSAL)	28	4	Legalized only in 2010
Tunisia	281	60%	National Agency for Employment and Independent Work (ANETI) Ministry of Vocational Training and Employment	91	2	Private agencies are illegal

Source: Diego F. Angel-Urdinola, Diego F., Arvo Kuddo, and Amina Semla. "Public Employment Agencies in the Middle East and North Africa." *Building Effective Employment Programs for Unemployed Youth in the Middle East and North Africa.* World Bank, 2010. Tables 1.1, 1.2 and 1.3

ᵃBeirut only.

Advancing Self-Service: Market-Driven Intermediation via Technology

All studies of job search point to the importance of multiple strategies to achieve the best result, with informal plus formal methods. One key element of a market-driven intermediation system is that individuals pursue self-search as one of the channels of seeking employment. The method pursued with more attention in the advanced countries of course is the internet, but smart phone technology is opening up the use of cell phones as well. Most evidence points to the more dominant use of the internet in job search in higher skilled professions, but this may change over the next decade. To the extent that self-search becomes more possible and more effective with the right intermediation tools such as labor market information systems, this permits scarce public resources to be employed at the institutional and policy levels for more entrenched employment challenges. OECD countries like Australia and the United Kingdom have spent years stimulating the private *market* for intermediation services with greater use of technology.

The Ta3mal network started in Egypt as a partnership between Microsoft and Silatech is a well-known non-governmental youth tech tool operating in the Middle East and North Africa. Ta3mal is a free web-based resource for young people – an example of a non-profit-private partnership, providing them with help in preparing a CV, career advice, and virtual advising. It includes both formal work and entrepreneurship.[54] With high rates of education in both the Middle East and North Africa, it is an example of a technology-driven instrument that is more applicable to the better educated in developing regions. Yet even in Africa, where rates of internet usage are low, albeit growing, experimentation is focusing on using cell phones as delivery and information agents.

Cell phone technology put into the hands of low-income beneficiaries is growing by leaps and bounds in Africa. The United Nations reports that Africa's annual growth *rate* of mobile subscriptions is the highest in the world, at 65%.[55] Well-known is M-Pesa, a mobile payment system first developed by the private mobile operating company Safaricom in Kenya, now spreading throughout Africa, Asia and Eastern Europe. By December 2011, it had 17 million Kenya subscribers in a country of 44 million.[56] Both M-Pesa and Ta3mal are examples of market-driven initiatives that expand the range of tools available to foster labor intermediation in developing countries without direction from the public sector but are able to coordinate and support public sector initiatives. Cell phone delivery of social policy cash transfer payments, for example, has greatly aided the regularity and predictability of payments in Africa.

Advancing Accountable Schools and Training Institutions

One of the more frequently cited disconnects in developing the technical and work-related skills needed for the workplace is the disconnect between what schools and training institutions deliver and what employers actually need. This is far more fundamental than just facilitating transitions from school and training to work, but goes more profoundly to the curriculums, teaching methods, and applicability of learning to the job. Here developing countries share similar challenges with the developed world, although the disconnect and the dimension of the problem is greater in the developing world – poorly schooled young people, dropouts, limited numbers of firms that train their workers, training programs in fields where there are no jobs, universities producing unemployable graduates, few options for adults to return to school or retool – shall I go on?

Skill development as it stretches from early childhood through schooling to university level throughout the lifecycle is the subject of many books, well beyond the scope of this one. But its interrelationship with job placement and intermediation is unavoidable. Expanding and improving the efficiency of job placement services moves in tandem with improving the articulation of skill demands and the link of schools and training institutions to the workplace. Remember back in Chapter 1, the surveys of employers worldwide say the talent shortage around the globe is growing while skill demands are generally increasing. One fundamental feature then of a better functioning national intermediation system is its role in building incentives or pressure for more accountable schools and training institutions.

This accountability is not built by a government program or regulations, but over time by the combination of market pressures (students going to schools that give better results and skills), good public and private incentives, social responsibility and in select cases as part of national skills boards or skills strategies (e.g. Malaysia, Singapore). The principal drivers for change are the institutions themselves. Accountability starts first with collecting and publically disclosing basic information and knowledge: where do our graduates get jobs? Do our curriculums prepare them well for the jobs of today, tomorrow? Accountability advances next to the institutional, curricular and systems changes needed to make accountability, performance and flexibility integral to the institution. What needs to change to better align what students are taught with the skills they need for employment? How do universities, schools, or training programs compare against each other? The implication is not that schools and universities teach only what is relevant to the workplace, but that students have the information and can choose more employment relevance if that is what they seek.

The evolving national intermediation system can play a host of supporting information roles with many different entrance doors. Romania has begun tracer studies of its university graduates, one of the many Eastern European countries looking at the problem of good rates of university graduation but with poor connections of these graduates to the labor market.[57] A university-based education to employment data system considered a global model is *Alma Laurea* begun in Italy in 1994. The website and associated programs now track 91% of Italy's graduates from 72 universities at 1, 3 and 5-year intervals.[58] High school students can get detailed information on employment, graduation, earnings, and skills of graduates in every school in the 72 university system. Foreign and Italian employers are now using the CV repository to search for skilled employees, with 400,000 CVs accessed in 2015. Under grant financing, *Alma Laurea* is now working with Turkey's universities to establish a similar system called THEQA. *Alma Laurea* is an example of the expansion of diverse private institutions that can grow to play an intermediary function on a national scale well outside the old lines of employment services. Advancing skill development and systems to certify just what skills have been acquired is yet another step. Skill standard systems will understandably take on a host of adaptations in diverse developing economies to shape very different multi-actor national intermediation systems. Given the premium placed on future labor markets on skills, my guess is that many more innovations and adaptations in late Stage 2 will come from the reform and advancement of education and training.

Human Resources Development as a Career: Fostering Networks, Societies, Education

On a smaller scale, the advancement of national labor intermediation systems will also require a more skilled cadre of job counselors and human resource professionals. In countries such as the United States, masters' degrees in human resources management are common and serve both for HR managers of large firms as well as those in private and public intermediation. For developing countries this means fostering a "market" of increasingly skilled professionals who can move between and among these growing numbers of intermediary firms, training institutions, and schools as well as the curriculums and training materials that fit local markets.

This area as well should be seen as a shared role with universities and training institutions, rather than offered solely via one service itself. Public and private employment agencies should be developing training modules which permit the skills advancement and certification of professionals "on the job". University or graduate-level training in career guidance, while very rare in developing countries, might be fostered through collaboration between universities and public agencies. Included should be professional societies, associations of job counselors who themselves can become agents to support skill and career development. Important for this evolution is to see human resources as a career path within intermediation services and among public, private and associated institutions with human resources and intermediation functions. An example of this multi-level professionalization of job counselors can be seen in Ireland, as follows:

- **Level 1**: Distance learning: one-year program, workshops of two days each with a certificate upon completion. Offered through public universities.
- **Level 2**: Two-year distance learning and practical program using cases of client job seekers. Offered through public universities.
- **Level 3**: Master's level program with greater emphasis on professional career guidance. Offered by one private university, Galway.[59]

Focusing on Growing Sectors/Jobs Strategies. . . . Towards Stage 3?

By now it is clearer that the three big-picture changes moving from employment to labor intermediation services (Stage 2) occur and interact in real time: creating new and linked services, improved management and efficiency, and the advancement of a national intermediation market. Attempts to script how the three interact would zap their ability to adapt to changing market needs, although it might make it easier to describe in this book!

If one were to attempt to direct the flow of the intermediation services tide, the most appropriate focus for developing countries in Stage 2 should be where it is needed most – in sectors where either employment is growing or future investment/employment is desired or predicted. This makes intuitive sense as this is where the greater consequences for more efficient hiring occurs – less time, better match of employee to job, more productive employees, and better articulation of skill needs. One more time, it is duly noted that good employment generation presents a fundamental obstacle in the developing world, of which intermediation plays just a small part.

Here the point is that innovation and expansion flows more naturally when focused on where better intermediation is needed. This focus could be on attracting or meeting new foreign or domestic investment or contributing to a wave – or even a ripple – of employment growth, be it in a region or sector.

There are two levels where the employment growth spotlight is worth considering. As a national intermediation system in Stage 2 is building through the three big-picture changes, the first level to examine is *local* and *regional*. Local and regional improvements in labor intermediation can have spillover effects expanding employment by improving the articulation of skill needs, bringing in new intermediation actors, and eventually being able to apply intermediation lessons in other sectors or nationally. An example from Mexico: Mexico's fundamental employment problem has been described as too large a cohort of low productivity labor in the middle, and too few high-end jobs.[60] Even in this environment, employment is growing in tourism in coastal areas but with problems. There is too much rotation and rotating poorly qualified workers making it difficult for the industry to be more competitive to deliver high-end service that require more workers more continuity and skill from air conditioning to refrigeration to waiters. In Riviera Maya, Mexico, the local hotel association, AHRM (*Asociacion Hoteleros de la Riviera Maya*) worked in partnership with the local vocational-technical institutions and public employment services and become an intermediary institution to place students in hotel jobs, create more varied types of internships and work orientation. The dynamic interaction is leading to curriculum changes and more stable hiring from local vocational-technical schools few of whom had previously been hired in the local industry. Fast forward, the collaboration on intermediation ended up setting in motion better articulation by the local industry of what they needed, an expansion of job listings nationally, and greater hiring of local young people who will more likely advance in technical careers in tourism.

This is a small example of where growing sectors can set in motion a range of interconnections between schooling, training, and jobs (Box 5.1).

The second, *national* level leads us to the final chapter. The lack of good jobs is a "problem" of very different dimensions and content between developing and middle-income economies. Not a rocket science-type revelation. However, this should lead us to thinking that integrating better intermediation in the new jobs agenda is and should take on a different character or path when applied to such diverse economies. Chapter 5 speculates, with some developing country examples moving in this direction, also about where intermediation might fit in the new development agenda for jobs. It postulates that a Stage 3 is emerging in which labor intermediation services become better integrated and interconnected not merely as a labor market policy but by playing a contributory role in workforce development, social and labor policy, and economic development.

NOTES

1. "Labour Migration for Employment – a Status Report for Nepal," Web March 9, 2016.
2. Omar S. Arias and Carolina Sánchez-Páramo, *Back to Work: Growing with Jobs in Europe and Central Asia*, 2014, p. 322.
3. David Card, Jochen Kluve, and Andrew Weber, "Active Labor Market Policy Evaluation: A Meta-Analysis," February 2009.
4. Gordon Betcherman, et al. "Impacts of Active Labor Market Programs," 2004.
5. Rita Almeida, Jere Behrman, and David Robalino, *The Right Skills for the Right Job*, 2012.
6. Diego F. Angel-Urdinola, Arvo Kuddo and Amina Semiali, *Building Effective Employment Programs for Unemployed Youth in the Middle East and North Africa*, p. 30.
7. *Turkey: Managing Labor Markets Through the Economic Cycle*, 2013.
8. Many other developing countries would label this short-term training as, in many other systems, vocational training refers to long skills courses and includes vocational-technical high schools. Turkey's program had a highly educated population and was not preparing trainees for careers in particular fields *per se.*
9. Saroljini Hirshleifer, David McKensie, Rita Almeida, and Cristobal Ridao-Cano, *The Impact of Vocational Training for the Unemployed*, March 2014.
10. *Ibid.*, p. 10.
11. Suzanne Dureya, Jacqueline Mazza, and Ferdinando Regalia, *Social and Labor Market Policies in Tumultuous Times: Confronting the Global Crisis in Latin America and the Caribbean*, 2009.

12. For a comprehensive review of East Asia policy responses see Gordon Betcherman and Islam Rizwanul, *East Asia: Issues and Policy Responses*, 1979.
13. *Migration and Remittances Factbook 2011*, World Bank, 2011, p. X. In the latter two corridors, some of this migration is related to border changes rather than physical migration.
14. *Ibid.*
15. Omar S. Arias and Carolina Sánchez-Páramo, *Back to Work: Growing with Jobs in Europe and Central Asia*, 2014, p. 371.
16. *Ibid.*, p. 11.
17. *In Search of Opportunities: How a More Mobile Workforce Can Propel Ukraine's Prosperity*, World Bank, 2012.
18. http://www.iskur.gov.tr/en-us/jobseeker/registration.aspx
19. Dovelyn Rannveig Agunias, "Regulating Private Recruitment in the Asia-Middle East Labour Migration Corridor,"August 2012.
20. *World Development Report: Jobs 2013*, World Bank, 2012.
21. A regional trade agreement with migration provisions covering the Southern Cone countries of South America: Argentina, Brazil, Chile, Bolivia and Paraguay.
22. Jacqueline Mazza and Eleanor Sohnen, *Crossing Borders for Work: New Trends and Policies in Labor Migration in Latin America and the Caribbean*, May 2012.
23. Yoonyoung Cho and Maddalena Honorati, *Entrepreneurship Programs in Developing Countries*, April 2013.
24. *Ibid.*, p. 32.
25. Erica Field, Seema Jayachandran, and Rohini Pande, "Do Traditional Institutions Constrain Female Entrepreneurship?" May 2010.
26. Diego F. Angel-Urdinola, Arvo Kuddo and Amina Semiali, *Building Effective Employment Programs for Unemployed Youth in the Middle East and North Africa,*, 2013.
27. Ranjula Bail Swain and Adel Varghese, "Delivery Mechanisms and Impact of Microfinance Training in Indian Self-Help Groups," January 2013.
28. *Ibid.*, 21.
29. Yoonyoung Cho and Maddalena Honorati, *Entrepreneurship Programs in Developing Countries*, April 2013, p. 32.
30. Jacqueline Mazza, *Unemployment Insurance: Case Studies and Lessons for Latin America and the Caribbean*, 1999.
31. *El Mundo del los Servicios de Empleo*, Executive Summary, 2015, p. 5.
32. *Turkey: Managing Labor Markets Through the Economic Cycle*, 2013, p. 14.
33. Diego F. Angel-Urdinola, Arvo Kuddo and Amina Semiali, *Building Effective Employment Programs for Unemployed Youth in the Middle East and North Africa*, p. 30.
34. *El Mundo del los Servicios de Emp leo*, Executive Summary, 2015, p. 9.
35. Christina Kappaz and Rosa Cavallo, *Case Studies: Mexican Employment Service*, 2009.

36. Johanna Poetzsch, *Case Management: the Magic Bullet for Labour Integration?*, 2007
37. *Op. Cit.*, p. 13.
38. Liivi Kaar, Indrek Motteus, and Elina Kulijus, "Estonian Unemployment Insurance Fund," 2014.
39. Scrivener et al., *National Evaluation of Welfare-to-Work Strategies*, 2001.
40. Howard Bloom, Carolyn Hill, and James Riccio, "Linking Program Implementation and Effectiveness: Lessons from a Pooled Sample of Welfare-to-Work Experiments," 2003.
41. Johan Vikstrom, Michael Rosholm, and Michael Svarer, "The Relative Efficiency of Active Labour Market Policy," 2011.
42. Jacqueline Mazza, *Fast Tracking Jobs*, 2011.
43. United Kingdom Commission for Employment and Skills, *2010 Employment Skills Almanac*, June 2010.
44. Gordon Betcherman, et al. "Impacts of Active Labor Market Policies," 2004.
45. Sang Hyon Lee, Comments at Seminar: Performance Management in Public Employment Services, March 19, 2015.
46. United Kingdom Commission for Employment and Skills, June 2010.
47. Daniel Finn, *Subcontracting in Public Employment Services*, 2011; Daniel Finn, *The Design and Effectiveness of Active Labor Market Policies in OECD Countries*, 2011.
48. Cost-benefit in intermediation systems has many complexities due to the multiple services and benefit series delivered over time and is thus less common. Analysis in OECD countries has typically focused on benefits related to reduced time collecting unemployment insurance.
49. *Ibid.*
50. Els Sol and Mies Westervald, *Contractualism in Employment Services*, 2005.
51. Daniel Finn, *Subcontracting in Public Employment Services*, 2011.
52. David Freud, *Decreasing Dependency, Increasing Opportunity*, 2007.
53. Sang Hyon Lee, Comments at Seminar Performance Management in Public Employment Services, March *19* 2015.
54. Peter Glick, et al. *The Private Sector and Youth Skills and Employment*, Rand Corporation, 2015.
55. UNDESA, "World Urbanization Prospects," 2014.
56. *The World of Public Employment Services*, 2015, p. 121.
57. Lars Sondergaard et al., *Skills Not Diplomas*, 2012.
58. http:/bi/www.almalaurea.it/en/info/chisiamo
59. Jacqueline Mazza, "*Estrategias Basados en Destrezas y Empleo*," Powerpoint Presentation, February 2011.
60. Consuelo Ricart, Tzitzi Moran, and Christina Kappaz, *Toward a National Framework of Lifelong Learning in Mexico*, 2014.

CHAPTER 5

A Stage 3? Labor Intermediation and the New Jobs Agenda for Development

Finally it has become fashionable to talk about jobs as central to development! Good, stable jobs are fundamental to getting the poor permanently out of poverty and poor countries permanently on the road to middle-income status. It is also no secret that to get anyone, and the poor in particular, a good job in a developing country requires many, many things to work in the right direction. This book has focused very practically on just one policy – labor intermediation services – that need to work right to support a more efficient, fair, and productive way to connect people to jobs. With examples from a wide range of developing countries, this book has taken you from the establishment of core employment service functions in Stage 1 through to advanced Stage 2 – an evolution, sometimes even a transformation, into labor intermediation services that can serve a diverse and relatively country-specific set of misconnections among employment, skills, training, education, and private sector growth. This chapter will go another step further to look at how labor intermediation services are working, and need to work, differently and in coordination with other policies to move workers to jobs in today's more global economies.

Labor intermediation services play a supportive, not the lead, policy role in the new jobs agenda. Even in advanced Stage 2, a single national employment service working with a wide range of partner institutions will likely only serve a proportion of new job hires. The United Kingdom's *Jobs Plus Service Centers*, for example, advanced in coordinating tailored

© The Author(s) 2017

J. Mazza, *Labor Intermediation Services in Developing Economies*,
DOI 10.1057/978-1-137-48668-4_5

interventions for the long-term unemployed, are estimated to serve directly only 20% of new job hires.[1] But, for developing countries with even less functional labor markets, there are indirect impacts of labor intermediation and much wider market changes to consider beyond just how many new hires are registered by a national intermediation service.

This book has argued that developing countries would be wise to look at the functioning and needs of the broader labor intermediation "system" for both setting national jobs priorities for services and for targeting what part of the market needs expansion. What is likely to be more significant for developing economies than strict placement rates are the indirect impacts of a better functioning labor market operating today with so little transparency in job hiring and so much dysfunction. Indirect impacts include inducing education and training systems to focus more on the placement of their graduates and stimulating a new generation of businesses in the business of intermediation. Placement rates are not going to be able to measure individual impacts such as those who found a different type of job based on better labor market information; employers improving who they hire, how openly they hire, and their productivity gains to better defining their skill needs. As Chapter 4 laid out, what may be more or at least just as consequential for developing countries is where the market itself can be stimulated to work on a more open and competitive basis and expanded via a chain of market-stimulating effects. A pro-jobs agenda in any country includes getting intermediation as part of a functional labor market right, or at the very least, a lot better.

If we are to imagine a Stage 3, it is not necessarily a bigger single national employment service once a level of scale has been reached. Instead, it would be that better labor intermediation – the matching of workers and their skills to employment – happens more significantly in multiple directions on multiple fronts by diverse "intermediaries" to contribute to more productive workers in better jobs. This includes training and educational institutions being induced to align their curriculums to actual jobs, foreign investment being linked more directly to jobs and career paths, and social policy better leading people from income supports out of poverty through employment exits. In short, better labor intermediation plays its role in a Stage 3 as part of a more strategic national focus on employment *as a component* of a wide spectrum of other policies and activities of distinct intermediaries, far beyond the initial conception of a single active labor market policy acting on its own.

This chapter concludes this book by speculating on how improved labor intermediation services can play a more integral role in development oriented to productivity and better job growth, integral roles appropriate to what labor intermediation can and cannot do, à la Chapter 2. To do so, we need to restate our labor market humility one more time. Tens of thousands of PhDs in economics have not been able to pinpoint what is needed to foster good job growth – if it had, the Nobel Prize Committee would have retired! What is humbly suggested here is that better labor market connections will not be made in an isolated, single-policy fashion in the new jobs agenda but will require stronger relationships with at least three other key policies: economic development, social and labor market policies, and skills development/education. Truth be told, this new more integrated policy direction on jobs is much more than speculation. Both developing and developed countries are moving to infuse, integrate, and connect labor intermediation to a wider set of policies. Is one direction better than another? Aren't all these interconnections needed?

While it is premature to assert a single global answer to where labor intermediation services should fit in a pro-jobs development agenda, put all your money on the bet that there is not one single answer. To help see what is worth betting on, this chapter looks in the window of some current new thinking and policy directions about, first, how different jobs strategies fit in different country contexts. From the vantage point of different countries/ different jobs agendas, we then recap the wider roles of labor intermediation services as "connectors," as looked at in Chapter 4. This can lead us finally to the policy future, a look at how labor intermediation services are and can be playing greater connector roles in a future Stage 3. This chapter examines future policy integration from three dimensions: integrating from the "center" with workforce, education and skills development (OK, a big simplification, but indulge me for this last chapter); from the "left" with social and labor market policy; and, finally, from the "right" with economic development. This is not pure speculation, but we can already see this policy experimentation under way in middle-income developing countries.

DIVERSE JOBS CHALLENGES MEAN DIVERSE JOBS STRATEGIES

A lot of sound, new thinking is starting from the idea that the "jobs problem" is actually quite different in different developing economies, and that the traditional policy solutions need some major overhauling and tailoring, may be with very different sets of leading policies, some even from left field. The traditional policies, all of which still play important roles in economic growth include: sound macroeconomic policies, good business climate, flexible labor market policies, open trade policies, a social protection and pension foundation, good education, the combination of active and passive labor market policies (including labor intermediation services) – whew, even that is overwhelming! It is not that this set of sound policies doesn't make sense, but that it isn't enough to catalyze what may be needed to make a country grow in a global world where its trading partners and competition is shifting simultaneous with the changing nature of employment. This set of sound policies that has guided development thinking does not translate directly into jobs strategies as we need to take into account wide variations in developing countries in resource endowments; in the age profile of populations; or, in the weakness or strength of their institutions, to name a few.

The World Bank's 2013 World Development Report on Jobs categorized a range of distinct jobs challenges in the developing world and looked at some relatively successful developing country cases to identify major overarching policies which are key to success for particular jobs challenges, as presented below in Table 5.1. It is not that other key factors and policies – traditional and non-traditional – were not also needed to work in coordination. What is more interesting is that the wide range of

Table 5.1 Diverse job challenges; diverse jobs strategies: Perspectives from the World Development Report

Type of jobs challenge	Key policies	Case example
Agrarian economy	Land reform; agriculture extension; market incentives	Vietnam
Urbanizing economy	Land-use planning; comprehensive urban planning	Korea
Resource-rich economy	Fiscal stability; export-oriented policies; social investment	Chile
Small island nations	Active use of return migrant agreements; linkages with key local economy(ies)	Tonga
Countries with high youth unemployment	Competition in trade markets through trade integration	Slovenia
Formalizing economies	Non-contributory programs (e.g. social, pensions); simplified rules and enforcement	Brazil
Aging populations	Disability and pension reform; higher retirement age	Poland

Source: Adapted from *World Development Report 2013: Jobs*, World Bank, 2012

key overarching policies and reforms stretch into such areas as land reform (Vietnam), urban planning (Korea) and migration policies (Tonga).

Even after organizing countries by their key jobs challenge, the argument is still not that one-policy-size-fits-all even within the same category. Similar agrarian economies may not be able to emulate Vietnam's success in a different regional market and a different set of human capital-building institutions; hence the focus in development today on developing more country-specific jobs strategies. With the exception of Tonga's focus on integrating return migrants, labor intermediation services or, more accurately, the labor intermediation system should be understood, as argued in this book, as playing a complementary, supportive role (not the primary one) in the mix of policies that advance employment and skill growth. Vietnam has maintained a series of employment centers throughout the country. Korea's public employment service, featured as an example in Chapter 3, did play a contributing role both in times of crisis and of growth.[2] It is in the context of a more dynamic focus on supporting employment and economic growth that new and wider roles for labor intermediation services can be seen in the future.

Jobs strategies for developing economies, as individual as they may need to be, interact on a larger global stage that affects an increasing percentage of national production. "Globalization" – the integration of national economies through the exchange of goods, services, finance, technology and people – is transforming the lives and jobs of virtually every individual and society around the world and in the process has become the most important economic development of the last half-century. World trade in goods and services grew from approximately $2 trillion in 1980, or 16% of global GDP, to $18 trillion in 2012, or 25.5% of GDP.[3]

NEW AND WIDER ROLES FOR LABOR INTERMEDIATION SERVICES

The traditional roles of employment services – helping make a better match faster of worker to job – are still amply relevant to contribute to greater productivity and economic performance in today's developing economies. Clearly changing, as reviewed extensively in this book, is both how this is being done in the modern, global economy and where it is being done and by whom, beyond, across, and within national borders. Letting go of 1960s' understandings about what it takes to improve the match of workers (their skills, education) to jobs means removing some walls between what were once thought to be the separate policy "silos" of active labor market versus education versus economic development versus social policies.

Developing countries should consider moving from basic employment services to labor intermediation services *not only* because there are limitations to how much job placement – even hidden in discouraged workers – can be achieved in developing economies *but also* because in today's economies job matching and placement (or the old policy of employment services) functions less and less in isolation as a distinct intervention. With rapid job change, greater skills needs, and questions about the quality and job relevance of basic and technical education and training nearly everywhere, good labor intermediation can or should be able to affect a wider range of policies. These include: what and how countries train or educate; how the private sector detects and signals its skill needs; and how workers can aim for and build better careers and paths out of poverty. It should be able to contribute to these changes through its incentives, its savings of time and costs to employers, its information and market signals. To put these modern roles in terms of "market failures" (e.g. in economics-speak), wider roles of labor intermediation services can be relevant, depending on different country contexts, to:

- promote labor mobility within nations to areas with greater job openings;
- facilitate labor mobility across borders and upon return from abroad;
- stimulate the growth of private and NGO intermediation markets, particularly to serve disadvantaged populations better with multiple interventions and systematic follow-up;
- speed the transition of workers to new and better employment; and
- reduce transitions from un, under and informal employment or idleness.

Integrating and Rethinking Labor Intermediation Services: Left, Right and Center

Today with global markets, rapidly changing competition, and more frequent job change in diverse national contexts, it's time to throw away any remaining one-size-fits-all policy rule books. This book started as a practical, hands-on approach to a changing one active labor market policy, and it will end that way as well. What is already well into its experimentation stage in both developing and developed countries is the infusion or integration of better labor intermediation as part of economic development, social and human capital (skills, education, training) and social and labor policy. How to do this? Here policy learning is crossing many North-South frontiers and back again.

In all three of the policy areas reviewed here, a new set of institutional lenses need to be applied. Advancing labor intermediation as part of a jobs agenda in a global age will require collaboration and linkage across public ministries and private sector organizations. These are institutions that are used to thinking: "this is someone else's job." Old-line labor ministries understood their mandate as specifically for workers and their trade unions and thus against employers. Labor ministries in most developing countries have suffered from years of politicization, poor levels of funding, and politicized staffing. Their traditional roles to mitigate labor conflict, particularly with unions, and regulate an increasingly small formal labor market often led to years of underinvesting in the employment departments of labor ministries. This was compounded in most developing countries when state-funded training institutions were set apart institutionally from labor ministries so that skills development was separated from employment. Economist Howard Rosen argues that getting labor ministries a "seat at the policy table" means modernizing the role of labor ministries to target improving labor productivity and employment.[4] A modernized role for labor ministries is needed to better connect labor intermediation to a larger employment, skills, and economic agenda.

Beyond its impact on economic growth, inflation, and employment and earnings, globalization has challenged the relevance and effectiveness of traditional public and private economic institutions, including both economic policies and the economic policy-making process, as well as the role of labor ministries. Developing countries are now far from the days of import substitution which offered national governments the luxury of conceiving of economic policies in the context of a purely "domestic vacuum." Today, developing country governments must consider global feedback effects, including how individual policies will affect the international competitiveness of their firms and workers. Likewise, concern over international competitiveness requires policymakers to be more sensitive to how labor policies affect other policies. This requires a higher level of policy coordination across government agencies.

Integration from the Center (Workforce Development/Education/Training/Skills)

The best place to see the emerging, more integrated role of labor intermediation (connecting people to work) is via the systems to improve human capital and skills. This tight connection is precisely because the main objective of improved skill development is to link first with immediate employment and then build a career over time. The more systematic preparation of the workforce over a person's lifetime is now more commonly called "workforce development." Workforce development seeks to connect the range of transitions building to career paths – school to work, learning on the job, work returning back to school. It can also be built within specific economic sectors, as will be discussed below as sectoral economic development. Workforce development involves the whole spectrum of education and training: from improved basic schooling through reforms to university education, including reforms and modernization to technical education, vocational training, short-term skills training, apprenticeships and basic work skills.

I am calling this integration from "the center" because the skills nature and content of work is so central to the quality of fitting the right worker to the right job. Surveys of skill mismatches have made clear that better aligning the skills of the workforce to labor market demand can reap gains in both employment and productivity. Countries with large labor forces show some of the biggest mismatches: Brazil (61%), India (58%) and Turkey (52%).[5] Poorly aligned training and education lie at the heart of skills mismatches, but they are not always correlated with poor quality education and low enrollment. The Europe and Central Asia (ECA) region has highly regarded grade-school education as well as some of the highest enrollment rates at all levels of education, including university-level education with the exception of a few lower-income countries like Uzbekistan and Azerbaijan. Nonetheless, skill shortages were reported by the region's major employers to be the second greatest constraint to growth after tax rates.[6]

It is hard to attract new investment, foreign or domestic, in better jobs without a well-developed labor force to match. Ireland, a country that used a national skills strategy in the 1990s to attract foreign investment in first hardware and then software, and to realign its secondary and university curriculums to emerging employer demands, has among the lower skills mismatches in Manpower's 2015 survey (11%), up though from 2% in 2014.[7]

Workforce development is multi-level; improving the curriculum and employment-related content of training and advanced education aids a better fit of a worker to a job, and in a feedback loop, employers learn more specifically about what skills they are looking for, improving both their hiring processes and their in-house training. As workforce development needs to correlate directly with local labor market demand, many large countries, such as the United States, approach it with distinct state-level workforce development councils and career pathways to in-demand professions. Advancing skills development at a national level through the reform and modernization of human capital institutions and the workplace has taken on a new impetus via national skills strategies around the globe. South Africa's National Skills Development Strategy 2011–2016, for example, promotes the growth of the FET (Vocational-Technical) Colleges, better workplace learning, and improved public sector delivery.[8]

It is more realistic to understand workforce development as a dynamic process to continually fit workers to increasing and deepening skill levels rather than a static one-time hiring decision from one service. Intermediation within workforce development is multi-point as well, with industry, public, and non-profit actors. Industry needs feedback to not only affect hiring, but also how jobs are defined and what qualifications are sought. As a small illustration only, Box 5.1 presents the tourist region of Riviera Maya south of Cancun, Mexico, which set out to try and reduce job rotation and get a better qualified workforce to serve an increasingly competitive tourism industry.

In Riviera Maya, the local hotel association found as they worked with both the major hotels and with local vocational-technical colleges, offering short courses, work shadowing and other learning methods for high school-level students in their hotels, they could influence and help modernize the curriculums, and get a more reliable (e.g. more willing to stay longer) stream of high school-level employees they had previously written off. The process also enabled employers to articulate better the new skill needs in areas like refrigeration and mechanics, standardizing their hiring better across the industry and sending signals to the local technical schools and universities about what the new competitive demands are in their industry.

Box 5.1 Riviera Maya, Mexico: Strategic Growth in Tourism, Integrating from the Right and Center

Riviera Maya, south of Cancun on the Yucatan Peninsula in Mexico, had a perhaps enviable problem in the developing world. By 2008, it was creating jobs fueled by foreign investment in large hotels on a beautiful stretch of beach close to less well-known Mayan ruins but far enough from the party-friendly all-inclusives in Cancun. The Riviera Maya hotel association, *Associación Hoteleros de Riviera Maya* (AHRM), knew the growth was unsustainable though. International tourism was becoming more competitive, European visitors were demanding higher-end services which meant more staff with higher

(continued)

Box 5.1 (continued)

levels of training, such as eco-friendly maintenance. But in 2008, the hotels were busing in low-skilled labor from poor areas of Mexico and job rotation was way too high. The local vocational-technical schools had such a poor reputation that they were not a source of hiring, and hotels were going it alone to hire any workers they could find; the public employment service only had an office in Cancun and wasn't serving their market.

The AHRM led a human capital development initiative with local voc-tech schools, large and small hotels, and the Education and Labor Ministries that is changing hiring and training in Riviera Maya and the industry's competitive position in the process. The key instruments of change include:

- **From the "Center"**: engagement with local vocational-technical schools to start changing curriculums and providing more work opportunities and job orientation for upper secondary students, including hotel staff visiting schools and school instructors coming to hotels. Key for international competitiveness, it is the leading local hotels in the region who have led the higher standards. What is being created is a dynamic workforce development process in which hiring practices (who, when, how) are changed *simultaneously* with changes in training methods and curriculum.
- **Multi-channel intermediation**: job-matching instruments and players both multiplied and diversified. The AHRM expanded its own intermediation service, listing jobs for hotels, referring candidates, and streamlining and improving hiring by developing standard job profiles so that job seekers could hunt among hotels and see how one job led to a career stream within the industry. The public sector opened a new office in Riviera Maya to attend to increased local demand. Links between internships and job placement happened more automatically. The hotels report they are getting better qualified candidates and are using upper secondary students in place of college graduates who were often the ones prone to higher job rotation.

(continued)

> **Box 5.1** (continued)
> - **From the "Right"**: Riviera Maya has kept up high growth levels, increasing dramatically investment and number of rooms while upgrading the quality of the workforce. Importantly, it is growing as a higher-end destination with less downturn in the low season which is enabling it to position itself well to maintain and continue this growth and add even more to new job creation. Riviera Maya now exceeds Cancun in hotel rooms and occupancy and is the leading tourism destination in Mexico.

Integration from Left (Social Services/Labor)

Better connections to work are also being linked in developing countries via the coordinated delivery of a range of social services for the poor. Social services to the poor can be many and can often be disjointed if delivered by different public agencies or donors. The social services can include basic income support, health, water subsidies, and housing support, among others. Social services are both a principal and consistent access point to the poor as well as a route to address many of the multiple barriers the poor face to employment. Poverty presents multi-barriers to getting a better job: living in poor neighborhoods with high transport costs to jobs; home and child care responsibilities that make it hard to be reliable; lack of basic work readiness and behavior skills; and proper clothing to start. As a result, there is a fundamental logic in insuring that non-labor market barriers to work are reduced simultaneously with helping the poor to find work, using the hook of services that the poor access regularly to bring them into contact with labor intermediation services and training.

Perhaps the best-known innovation in social policy for developing economies is the conditional cash transfer programs, first pioneered by *Bolsa Familia* in Brazil and Solidarity now *Opportunidades* in Mexico. These conditional cash transfer programs (CCTs) gave typically monthly income support to the poor on condition of school attendance and health visits for the children of receiving families. They have demonstrated results in the incidence and depth of poverty, increased school attendance, and in some cases, better health.[9] Based on impact evaluations from Mexico and Brazil, a generation of CCTs and then unconditional cash transfers (CTs) beginning in largely low-income African countries is spreading throughout the developing world in many different varieties. What has been harder to achieve are sustainable labor market exits from such social programs. Specifically, once children graduate from school they enter labor markets where it is still hard to find or connect with quality employment and poverty can be reinserted.

Integrating or linking intermediation from the metaphorical left door, social assistance to the poor, is intended to help insure that social assistance is combined or linked to an actual transition into the labor market, the only feasible strategy to move the poor out of poverty. How to best link or integrate social and labor services is an evolving and still experimental policy field because of its complexity. Three different principal approaches to integrating social and labor services with intermediation in the developing and emerging economies are reviewed here; all three, however, show that connecting the poor, particularly the extreme poor, with work sufficient to keep them out of poverty is complex and depends on many quality-related services working well together. The most comprehensive social service integration type was developed by Chile in its program of coordinated social service delivery for the extreme poor. It is considered the most comprehensive program of its type because of the range of social services coordinated. It does this while also concentrating on the poorest of the poor, those living on typically $1.25/day). Through its program known as *Chile Solidario* (Chile Solidarity), Chile has made strides in reducing both poverty and extreme poverty. The origin of this approach came as Chile was growing but saw particularly in 1996–2003 that extreme poverty seemed entrenched, resistant to both economic growth and traditional social policy. The idea was to enable a more individual family approach which analyzed family needs and insured that beneficiary families received all the eligible and needed assistance to transition out of poverty. There were clear indications that the extreme poor, in particular, were unaware of the benefits they were eligible for, or had neither the time nor knowledge to access these benefits. To do this, Chile developed a "bridge" program to provide specialized social counselors who would help identify family needs, give priority access to a wide range of social services and guarantee receipt of all eligible social subsidies. The program strives to guide families out of poverty through the combination of cash assistance and improved investments in human capital and in income generation. Families were paid declining monthly benefits for two years, conditional on seeing these counselors, and then they could stay an additional three years in the program. For employment, priority access included access to training, self-employment programs and the local municipal employment services offices (known as OMILs in Spanish, translated as Municipal Offices of Labor Intermediation). Evaluations demonstrated that during the two years of specialized intervention via counselors, the extreme poor did have higher rates of participation in training, self-employment and job search programs. While an early impact evaluation showed a small gain in employment, the gains were limited by the availability and quality of both training and employment services.[10] In terms of lessons for inter-sectoral interventions on employment, another impact evaluation concluded similarly that the small employment outcome was "due in part to deficiencies in the public supply of training, micro-entrepreneurship and labour intermediation programmes, which are illustrative of the significant institutional challenges faced by a public policy that posits an intersectoral approach."[11] The program overall showed income gains but not much from employment – it seem that alot of the increase in family income came from the fact that more than one person in the household may be working. Education and health outcomes important for human capital development improved.[12] The disappointing employment results offer lessons for many countries on the need to learn how to deliver higher quality intermediation for the most difficult clients, the extreme poor. Self-employment programs in particular, frequently offered to rural clients, have shown short-term income gains, but have not evolved as strong enough employment strategies to overcome extreme poverty (see Chap. 4).

A second social policy integration approach is to provide or link job readiness/training services directly for those in CCT/CT-receiving families, either young people close to working age or working-age parents. None of the current approaches for exiting or graduating from CCTs or CTs is conditional on accepting assistance in searching or training for a job, as can be found in some unemployment insurance programs. One of the difficulties in constructing incentives for labor market exits with CCTs/CTs is the fear (justified or not) among some beneficiaries that their benefits will be cut if they become formally employed, or that jobs among their cohorts are too unstable. Colombia runs a series of graduation-type programs associated with its CCT recipients, including youth training, *Jovenes en Acción (Youth in Action)*, and a wage subsidy program (40% of the minimum wage for each low-income worker hired) run by the Social Development Ministry. It is more common to find social development ministries that try to add on employment components to social assistance rather than programs that link their programs to national employment services. CCT beneficiary direct links are more often found with national training programs such as in Brazil. Some CCT/CT programs look to "add on" a labor intermediation component to the final phases of the CCT, e.g. when young people are close to finishing school. These are often small programs or even one-off job fairs with a social service orientation that, at best, are connected to only a few local employers. This book, and many others, have made the point that, for the poor to be systematically connected with better employment, they need to be connected with national labor intermediation services that serve a broader range of jobs. It is only by offering a range of employment, by connecting with a range of employers offering better quality employment, that the dynamic of moving up the poor both with employment and with social services can be set in motion. I have seen small job-finding services attached to community-based social services, but they rarely work well for the poor unless the intermediation function is accomplished by someone or some service with a more private sector orientation. Employers will know soon enough to come to that service only to get the least qualified. When specialized intermediation does work well for the poor, as in *Galpão Aplauso* in Rio de Janiero and Youth Build (Chap. 4), it is when the right placement director has the right contacts and knows which doors to knock on. That is, a placement service with established credibility with employers.

A third approach is the co-location of the delivery of social services with a national labor intermediation service, either physically or virtually. This is intended to ease and increase access for the poor. The ILO (International Labour Organization) is piloting a "single window service" in Cambodia and Indonesia combining social service delivery and employment services. It is to be implemented via sub-national and local centers, using technology such as smart cards and fingerprint identification to ease access to services.[13] Estonia has one of the most sophisticated E-platforms for labor market information, social services, and employment services. The integration of social and labor market programs was phased in, beginning in 2009 with the Estonia Labor Market Board (the employment/intermediation service) taking over responsibility for the Unemployment Insurance Fund. The integration is not just virtual, but involved staff changes, shifts in bureaucratic responsibilities, and bringing in a more IT-savvy board. The social and labor policy integration was implemented within a much larger set of E-government service reforms of the Estonian government. The Estonians maintain that their business model is based on more individual attention, with more "intensive and effective" job intermediation, benefits and services "well on time," with an employment focus on "individual needs not wishes or risks."[14]

Integration from the Right (Economic Development/Strategic Sectors)

Finally, particularly promising from the standpoint of a focus on employment demand and better quality jobs are interventions that integrate intermediation and employment in economic development strategies. There are many forms in play in both developed and developing countries. Two of interest are national economic development strategies and sectoral economic interventions.

National economic development strategies are typically economy-wide strategies, and for developing economies often seek to attract and channel foreign and domestic investment to promote economic growth. Those integrating human capital interventions to stimulate both employment and economic growth strategy are of particular note here. Ireland built their growth strategies in the 1990s through attracting foreign investment and then quickly realigning education to produce the next generation of higher technology products – from call centers, to computer hardware, to software. Realignment of secondary, vocational-technical, and higher education was aided by an Expert Group on Skills.[15] In Ireland's case, the National Employment Service increased operations and job matching of both returning Irish migrants and Eastern European migrants.[16] Singapore prioritized STEM (Science, Technology, Engineering and Math) skills at all levels of education, benchmarked to international standards, and used web-based career information, catapulting from its low rankings in 1960 to the number two ranking by the Global Economic Forum for Global Competitiveness in Higher Education and Training (2014).[17] Malaysia is a third developing country that leapt forward in growth, also using an entity to help calibrate and realign education and training with employment demand. There are some common success factors in these three cases of smaller economies, as noted by Monika Aring of SkillsNation:[18]

- a national strategic vision or articulated national plan;
- a medium-term human capital strategy, including planning for future skill needs, training incentives in STEM fields;
- benchmarking to international standards;
- an independent human resource agency that can calibrate the supply and demand of skills;
- realigned education delivery with adequate resources.

In the three cases of Malaysia, Singapore and Ireland, it is important to point out that existing intermediation services played supporting and enabling roles, rather than leadership ones. In all three cases, some form of new independent skills agency was created to benchmark key needed skills and induce universities and training institutions to produce graduates in these fields. Such independent agencies were able to cross new institutional lines, but did so with a set of competencies in skill identification, educational and training curriculums and industry needs that would not be the typical skill set of an intermediation service. In the case of Ireland's Expert Group on Future Skill Needs, both national and international experts served on its board, and detailed studies were prepared in new and emerging employment fields, such as green jobs and information processing that were used by the counselors of the National Employment Service to guide career advice.

Sectoral strategies are defined as "partnerships of employers within one industry that bring government, education, training, economic development, labor and community organizations together to focus on the workforce needs of an industry within a regional labor market."[19] There are many variants of sectoral strategies, spanning distinct industries and suppliers as well as ones with distinct geographic reach. Groups of industries can be formally developed into supply-chain clusters, or drawn naturally together via geographic co-location "agglomeration" strategies, as in Mumbai, India. A random-assignment evaluation of three sectoral strategies in the United States found increases in employment, significant increases in earnings (18% more over two years) and better quality employment.[20] By channeling employment into growth sectors, more people worked more consistently at higher wages with more benefits.[21] The Colorado, US-based Aspen Institute studied these sectoral strategies further and found that 48% of the previously poor participants exited poverty as a result solely of better income.[22] Like workforce development strategies, sectoral strategies seek to address current and future skill needs by aligning institutions better to address those needs, helping employers better define and develop skill needs and using labor market information to guide this realignment.

While integrating intermediation systems directly with employment strategies or growing sectors seems clearly the most promising direction for future intermediation evolution, which economic/employment strategies countries should follow when is far from an international consensus. Economist Dani Rodrik argues that the days of export-led growth pursued by East Asian nations is unlikely to fit future cases. He argues for "contextual analysis" for individual countries as the context continues to change both within and outside a country. In "One Economics, Many Recipes" he argues that countries must both experiment and adapt, as China did with a dual-track agricultural reform and manufacturing boom and Mauritius did with industrialization.[23] In a recent forum, Dr. Rodrik presented three types of economic growth "channels," each with distinct short and longer-term implications for employment:[24]

1. **Fundamental Channel**. This is the most well-known channel or strategy. It is based on a progressive transformational change in human capital investment and skills upgrading together with major institutional change. Rodrik argues this is a slow strategy, sometimes taking a generation, but it is an essential channel for sustainable, long-term growth.
2. **Escalator Channel**. This "big leap" strategy Rodrik argues has a bigger short-term impact on growth but less on employment over the medium term.
3. **Structural Change Channel**. In this well-known channel, successful developing countries are making a structural advance out of low-productivity agriculture to higher-productivity, export-oriented manufacturing. In such cases, Rodrik argues you only need policy reform in one key sector as is the approach pursued by South Korea, Singapore, Taiwan, Malaysia, and China. With China's slowdown and its impact on other developing countries, many economists wonder if this export-led manufacturing strategy can really be replicable for other countries.

Are we currently seeing the end of the export-led growth in the manufacturing model? With the greatest growth rates now in the services sector, and from resource-led growth (e.g. Latin America, Africa), do these require specialized attention despite the lower numbers of jobs associated with these sectors? India, which is growing in a healthy manner but principally in services, offers some pause for thought. India may be signaling at least a different path for advancing labor productivity, essentially continuing both low-productivity agriculture and a small, low-productivity manufacturing sector. Whether India can advance by skipping over manufacturing-dominated growth and pursing labor productivity growth principally in services, such as in information technology and finance, is far beyond the scope of this book. The future for matching workers to growing employment areas will lie in matching workers to jobs more rapidly, many more times over one working life, and with higher skill and technological content – whatever sectors, products or value chains are producing employment – is more widely agreed on for the future of both developing as well as developed economies.

MORE JOB CHANGE, MORE OFTEN WITH MORE SKILL CONTENT: THE FUTURE OF LABOR INTERMEDIATION

The future of the "how" of the delivery of better labor intermediation has been evolving to a wider spectrum of public-private-NGO intermediation services progressively in stages with more recent linkages, as laid out in this chapter, from the right, center or left with workforce/skills, social, and economic development policies. But this represents just one plane in which the future of labor intermediation services is changing. The other is the "what" and the "how often" – labor intermediation will be taking place in more globalized world economies more often and with the need for greater skill articulation than ever before.

More Rapid Job Change with More Transitions/Greater Range of Clients

Early employment services in the United States and Europe were conceived with the idea of getting the unemployed back into the labor market with the likelihood that they would continue in that job or career till retirement. Even when the mandate expanded to youth, there was little conception that these would be repeat clients. The rapid pace of job change, plus the multiplication of transitions between employment states have been amply documented and has changed the nature of the intermediation job of the future.[25]

Just a single worker in today's global economy, regardless of country of origin, can anticipate transitions from school to work, from potentially specialized training to work, from periods of unemployment and idleness to work, periods between jobs, and particularly in developing countries, migration between jobs within the same country and across borders. While not all these transitions will require assistance, the pace of job change and multiplicity of transitions will put bigger demands on all forms of intermediation in the future.

The job of intermediation will require more skill and more knowledge of the labor market than ever before, but will also require an understanding of how to apply this knowledge to a greater range of clients and different labor market pressures. Among the many changes globally is the changing demographic profile of many labor markets. In the advanced and many transition countries, the population is aging and, without adequate pensions or social protections, people will be working longer or adjusting to part-time or other forms of contract employment. A "youth bulge" is more characteristic of many developing economies, being particularly severe in the Middle East and North Africa.

Labor Mobility and Migration

Particularly in developing countries, the more global labor force is more mobile as well. As documented in Chapter 1, migration is an increasing feature of developing economies. Migration between developing countries is increasing more than from South to North. Chapter 4 detailed the range of ways that labor intermediation services have been developing to facilitate migration and, potentially, incorporate migration in a cycle of human capital improvements. This includes specialized temporary or curricular migration programs and return migration programs, particularly those linked with investments in migrant-sending communities.

Advancing Skill Content of All Work

Even more fundamental shifts are occurring in the skill content of work globally. Manufacturing employment has changed dramatically with a decreasing need for low and repetitive skills. The skill content of manufacturing as well as services is extended to higher-order skills, problem-solving and interpersonal skills, and greater levels of literacy and numeracy skills. These changes in employment come in the context of more technology and communications-driven economies. The key structural transformations needed in developing economies out of low-productivity agriculture require a human capital transformation via skills development, but for low-income developing countries the challenge is now even greater, given the higher skill content in future employment. The international consulting firm, Deloitte, estimates that the half-life of technology skills (the time period in which half the skills will become no longer marketable) is just 2.5–5 years, signaling the need for continual retooling in this key skill area.[26]

All the evidence to date is that the world economy is not adjusting well enough or quickly enough to the demands for higher-order skills. Surveys of skills mismatches demonstrate that mismatches are continuing to increase.[27] The World Bank reports that in developing and emerging economies skills constraints to growth are considered more acute now than in the first half of the 2000s. As documented in Graph 1.3, skills mismatches are as acute in key developing countries as in the advanced economies. Peru and Hong Kong have skill shortages over 60% – that is, 60% of employers say they can't find skilled workers to fill positions, similar levels to Japan (Chap. 1). Brazil and India, among the largest developing economies, have among the highest levels of skill shortages, which are great constraints to growth.[28] In addition to the efficiency losses that come from skills mismatches, there are groups that are affected more disproportionately. Skills mismatches are particularly affecting the ability of part-time workers, the young, and migrants to adjust to the labor market.[29]

According to the Institute for the Future, in the coming decade the global work force will require ten higher-order skills that are less explicitly taught today:[30]

1. **Sense-making**. The ability to determine deeper meaning or significance of what is being expressed (or the kind of skills machines are not good at).
2. **Social intelligence**. The ability to connect to others in a deep and direct way.
3. **Novel and adaptive thinking**. Proficiency at thinking and coming up with solutions beyond those that are rule-based.
4. **Cross-cultural competency**. Ability to operate in different cultural settings.
5. **Computational thinking**. Ability to translate vast amounts of data into abstract concepts and to understand data-based reasoning.
6. **New media literacy**. Ability to critically assess and develop content that uses new media forms, and to leverage these media for persuasive communication.
7. **Transdisciplinarity**. Literacy in and ability to understand concepts across multiple disciplines.
8. **Design mindset**. Ability to represent and develop tasks and work processes for desired outcomes.
9. **Cognitive load management**. Ability to discriminate and filter information for importance.
10. **Virtual collaboration**. Ability to work productively, drive engagement, and demonstrate presence as a member of a virtual team.

The advancing skill content of work is clearly placing more demands on increasing the skills of employment counselors, far beyond the typical profiling of a job seeker's skills to a more sophisticated measurement and detection of "soft" skills, interpersonal skills, including skills developed informally. It also depends on higher quality and more sophisticated labor market information systems and profiling and career guidance tools. Hungary's public employment service advanced in creating a nationwide career guidance and development system only by cutting across institutional and policy lines (Box 5.2).

Box 5.2 Hungary: Advancing a Career-Development/Guidance System in a Skills-Driven Economy
A decade ago, Hungary faced institutional fragmentation across its various agencies responsible for education, employment and training; this kind of fragmentation is something that most countries, developing and very developed, can relate to. As in many other countries, disparate responsibilities along the lifecycle of any individual meant information and guidance for identifying and then carrying out careers was piecemeal and fragmented as well. As a result, both young people and adults in Hungary had few tools to really plan, consult, or receive guidance in building jobs, training and education into careers.

From 2008 to 2010, the public employment service of Hungary, *Nemzeti Folalkoztatási Sozlagála*, invested heavily, along with support from the European Social Fund, in creating a nationwide career development guidance system. Using a new methodology, they built a consolidated career guidance system that crossed all the major sectors, providing both guidance, web resources and information. The Hungarian system built upon a range of European experience and also linked, via labor market information systems, to the European Union. The new career development/guidance system included the mapping of all current career guidance professionals across the myriad institutions – schools, vocational and technical education, adult education, universities, community-based services as well as the public employment service. It extended training for career development professionals, established a new career guidance network of professionals and established a life guidance portal, www.epalya.hu.
Source: http://www.epalya.hu/ The World of Public Employment Services, 2015, p. 95–96

Labor intermediation in the new global economy goes well beyond a matching function, and extends to aiding more efficient transitions, to linkage with human capital and skill development, enhancing the ability of developing countries to advance skill development as demanded by current economic trends. The contribution of labor intermediation services to these growing demands will depend on if, and how well, developing countries can create basic employment services that can grow into labor intermediation services in a Stage 2 relevant for the specific developing economy.

INTERMEDIATION ON A MORE DYNAMIC, GLOBAL STAGE

Looking into a crystal ball with a vision into the next five, ten and then twenty years, one might see an ever more active labor intermediation field crossing the developing, middle-income and advanced economies. This field would be building Stage 3 in multiple directions. National labor intermediation systems would be advancing in their varied private, public, NGO, trade union-affiliated forms. Simultaneously, we would likely see labor intermediation "embedded" in new policy linkages via workforce and skills development (from the center), social and labor market policy (from the left), and economic development (from the right). Which of these three dominates will likely have more to do with how countries construct their lead policies and which institutions see their futures advanced through collaboration. For developing countries, educational, training institutions and labor ministries may remain weak and entrenched unless they align and reform closer with performance and skills, and enlightened national leaders see the future tied to a better performing workforce. The private sector subject to ever greater global competition must embrace the change needed in how to train, hire, and develop the workforce.

The future will put more of a premium on the pace and innovation of labor market intermediation tools in a rapidly changing global marketplace with skill levels climbing. That is why it is high time to shed ideas of employment services as a single active labor market policy of a single national government and move to a more dynamic, market-driven vision of a labor intermediation system running multiple and interconnected sets of services and linkages to national policies and local institutions. I leave you here with the future well in progress. George and Ira Gershwin's song first came out in 1937. Their song "Nice Work if You Can Get it" will need to be put on hyper-overdrive by 2037, replayed within regions, across borders, and repeatedly over lifetimes.

NOTES

1. Alex Nunn, comments at Labor Intermediation Seminar: Performance Management in Public Employment Services, March 19, 2015.
2. Sang Hyon Lee, comments at Labor Intermediation Seminar: Performance Management in Public Employment Services, March 19, 2015.
3. International Monetary Fund, *World Economic Outlook*, accessed October 2013.
4. Howard Rosen, "Getting a Seat at the Policy Table," 2014.
5. Manpower Inc., *Talent Shortage Survey*, 2015.
6. Lars Sendergaard, et al. *Skills Not Just Diplomas*, World Bank, 2012, p. 2–3.
7. *Ibid.*
8. Department of Higher Education and Learning, *South Africa National Skills Development Strategy III*, 2012.
9. Romulo Paes-Souza, Fernando Regalia, and Marco Stampini, *Conditions for Success in Implementing CCT Programs*, 2013.
10. Osvaldo Larranaga et al. "Impact Evaluation of Child Solidario" *Journal of Latin American Studies*, 2012.
11. *Ibid.*
12. Emanuela Galasso, "Alievating Extreme Poverty in Chile," June 2011.
13. "The Single Window Service in Asia and the Pacific: Piloting Integrated Approaches to Social Protection Floors," International Labour Organization Fact Sheet, 2014.
14. Liivi Kaar, Indrek Motteus, and Elina Kuljus, "EUIS: Estonian Unemployment Insurance Fund," Powerpoint Presentation, 2014 and www.evonline.ee.
15. Monika Aring, "Autonomy or Collaboration?" 2014.
16. Jacqueline Mazza, "Estrategias basados en Destrezas y Empleo," Powerpoint Presentation, February 2011.
17. Number two out of 144 countries in 2012, as quoted in Aring, "Autonomy or Collaboration?" 2014.
18. *Ibid.*
19. *Sector Strategies: Coming of Age: Implications for State Workforce Policymakers.* National Governors' Association, Center for Best Practices, 2011.
20. Sheila Maguire, et al. *Tuning into Local Labor Markets: Findings from Sectoral Employment Study Public/Private Ventures, 2010.*
21. *Ibid.*
22. *Op Cit.*
23. Dani Rodrik. *One Economics: Many Recipes, 2007*, p. 164–67.

24. Dani Rodrik, presentation at World Bank conference, "New Growth Strategies: Delivering on Their Promise," October 14, 2015.
25. OECD Employment Outlook, 2014.
26. "Global Human Capital Trends", Deloitte, 2015.
27. Manpower Group, *Global Talent Survey 2015*, Manpower Group, 2015.
28. *Ibid.*
29. World Economic Forum, *Matching Skills and Labor Market Needs*, 2014.
30. Institute for the Future, *Future Work Skills 2020*, 2011.

BIBLIOGRAPHY

Adolfo Garcia, Gustavo, and Catia Nicodemo. *Job Search, Wage Inequality, and Neighborhood Channels in Developing Countries: The Colombian Case.* Bonn, Germany: Institute for the Study of Labor (IZA), Discussion Paper No. 7336, April 2013.

"*Alma Laurea*". Bologna, Italy: Alma Laurea Website, cited December 1, 2015. https://www.almalaurea.it/en/info/chisiamo

Almeida, Rita, Jere Behrman, and David Robalino. *The Right Skills for the Job? Rethinking Training Policies for Workers.* Washington, DC: The World Bank, 2012.

Angel-Urdinola, Diego F. *Labor Policy to Promote Good Jobs in Tunisia.* Directions in Development. Washington, DC: The World Bank, 2014.

Angel-Urdinola, Diego F., Arvo Kuddo, and Amina Semlali. *Building Effective Employment Programs for Unemployed Youth in the Middle East and North Africa.* Directions in Development. Washington, DC: The World Bank, 2013.

Arias, Omar, and Carolina Sanchez-Paramo. *Back to Work: Growing With Jobs in Eastern Europe and Central Asia.* Europe and Central Asia Reports. Washington, DC: The World Bank, 2014.

Aring, Monika. "Autonomy or Collaboration? An Examination of the Role of Labor Ministries in the Skills-Growth Strategies of Ireland, Malaysia and Singapore" (unpublished report). Washington, DC: Interamerican Development Bank, October 2014.

Betcherman, Gordon, Karina Olivas, and Amit Dar. *Impacts of Active Labor Market Programs: New Evidence from the European Commission Mutual Learning in*

© The Author(s) 2017
J. Mazza, *Labor Intermediation Services in Developing Economies,*
DOI 10.1057/978-1-137-48668-4

Developing and Transition Countries. Washington, DC: Social Protection Unit, The World Bank, January 2004.

Betcherman, Gordon, and Rizwanul Islam. *East Asian Labor Markets and the Economic Crisis: Impacts, Responses, & Lessons.* Washington, DC: The World Bank and the International Labour Organization, 2001.

Betcherman, Gordon, Amit Dar, Amy Lunistra, and Makota Ogawa. *Active Labor Market Programs: Policy Issues for East Asia.* Washington, DC: World Bank, Social Protection Paper No. 0005, January 2000.

Blázquez, Maite. *Skills-based Profiling and Matching in PES.* Brussels: European Commission, The European Commission Mutual Learning Program for Public Employment Services, November 2014.

Bloom, Howard, Carolyn Hill, and James Riccio. Linking Program Implementation and Effectiveness: Lessons from a Pooled Sample of Welfare-to-Work Experiments. *Journal of Policy Analysis and Management* 22 (4), 2003.

Brown, Alessia JG, and Johannes Koettl. Active Labor Market Programs – Employment Gain or Fiscal Drain? *IZA Journal of Labor Economics*: 4–12, 2015.

Calero, Carla, Veronica Gonzalez, Jochen Kluve, and Carlos Henrique Corseuil. *Can Arts-Based Interventions Improve Labor Market Outcomes for Youth? Evidence from a Randomized Trial in Rio de Janeiro.* Washington, DC: Interamerican Development Bank, 20 May 2014.

Card, David, Jochen Kluve, and Andrea Weber. Active Labor Market Policy Evaluations: A Meta-Analysis. *The Economic Journal* 120 (548): 452–77, November 2010.

Cho, Yoonyoung, and Maddalena Honorati. *Entrepreneurship Programs in Developing Countries: A Meta-Regression Analysis.* Washington, DC: World Bank, Human Development Network, Policy Research Working Paper 6402, April 2013.

Connecting People with Jobs. Paris: Organization for Economic Cooperation and Development (OECD) Publishing, 2014.

Contreras, Dante, Diana Kruger, Marcelo Ochoa, and Daniela Zapata. *The Role of Social Networks in Employment: The Case of Bolivia.* Santiago, Chile: University of Chile, Department of Economics, SDT 251, July 2007.

"Countries Where Poverty Rates Increased by Heads of Households Working in Temporary, Interim or Part-Time Work," in *World Social and Economic Development Outlook.* International Labour Organization [database online]. Geneva, Switzerland: Available from http://www.ilo.org/global/about-the-ilo/multimedia/maps-and-charts/WCMS_369630/lang--en/index.htm (accessed December 15, 2015).

Dureya, Suzanne, Jacqueline Mazza, and Ferdinando Regalia. *Social and Labor Market Policies for Tumultuous Times: Confronting the Global Crisis in Latin America and the Caribbean.* Washington, DC: Interamerican Development Bank, 2009.

Field, Erica, Seena Jayachandran, and Rohini Pande. Do Traditional Institutions Constrain Female Entrepreneurship? A Field Experiment on Business Training in India. *American Economic Review: Papers and Proceedings* 100 (2): 125–129, May 2010.

Fields, Gary S. *Working Hard, Working Poor.* New York: Oxford University Press, 2011.

Finn, Dan. *The Design and Effectiveness of Active Labor Market Policies in OECD Countries: A Review of Recent Evidence for Latin American and Caribbean Countries.* Washington, DC: The Inter-American Development Bank 2011.

———. *Subcontracting in Public Employment Services: Review of Research Findings and Literature on Recent Trends and Business Models.* Brussels, Belgium: The European Commission Mutual Learning Program for Public Employment Services, European Union DG for Employment, Social Affairs and Inclusion, 2011.

———. The 'Welfare Market' and the Flexible New Deal: Lessons from Other Countries. *Local Economy* 24 (1): 38–45, 2009.

Flores-Lima, Roberto. *Innovaciones en la Evaluación de Impacto del Servicio de Intermediación Laboral en Mexico.* Washington, DC: Inter-American Development Bank, Technical Note IDB-TN-118, April 2010.

———. *Una Evaluación de Impacto del Servicio de Empleo de la Ciudad de Mexico.* Washington, DC: Inter-American Development Bank, 2005.

Freud, David. *Reducing Dependency, Increasing Opportunity: Options for the Future of Welfare-To-Work.* Leeds, England: UK Department of Works and Pensions, 2007.

Future Work Skills: 2020. Palo Alto, CA: the Institute for the Future for the University of Phoenix Research Institute, 2011.

Galasso, Emanuela. Alleviating Extreme Poverty in Chile: The Short-Term Effects of Chile Solidario. *Estudios De Economia* 38 (1): 101–27, June 2011.

Gatti, Roberta. *Jobs for Shared Prosperity.* Washington, DC: The World Bank, 2013.

Glick, Peter, Crystal Huang, and Nelly Meija. *The Private Sector and Youth Skills and Employment Programs in Low- and Middle-Income Countries.* Santa Monica, CA: The Rand Corporation, 2015.

Global Employment Trends for Youth: 2015: Scaling up Investments in Decent Work for Youth. Geneva: International Labour Organization, 2015.

Global Human Capital Trends 2016: the New Organization: Different by Design. New York: Deloitte University Press, 2015.

Gregg, Paul, and Jonathan Wadsworth. How Effective are State Employment Agencies, Jobscentre Use and Job Matching in Britain? *Oxford Bulletin of Economics and Statistics* 58 (3): 443, 1996.

Hirshleifer, Sarojini, Rita Almeida, David McKenzie, and Cristobal Ridao-Cano. *The Impact of Vocational Training for the Unemployed.* Washington, DC: The World Bank, 2014.

Ibarrarán, Pablo, and David Rosas Shady. Evaluating the Impact of Job Training Programs in Latin America: Evidence from IDB Funded Operations. *Journal of Development Effectiveness* 1 (2): 195–216, 2009.

International Monetary Fund. *World Economic Outlook*. Washington, DC: International Monetary Fund, 2013 [cited October/15 2013].

Jobs for the 21rst Century: Indonesia Assessment. U.S. Agency for International Development, March 2007.

Liivi Kaar, Indrek Motteus and Elina Kuljus. "EUIS: Estonian Unemployment Insurance Fund". Unpublished Powerpoint Presentation, 2014.

Lee, Sang Hyon. Presentation at Labor Intermediation Seminar: Performance Management in Public Employment Service, Washington, DC: Inter-American Development Bank, March 19, 2015.

Kappaz, Christina, and Rosa Cavallo. *Case Studies: Mexican Public Employment Service*. Washington, DC: Inter-American Development Bank, 2009.

Kluve, Jochen. The Effectiveness of European Active Labor Market Programs. *Labour Economics* 17, 13 February 2010.

Labour Migration for Employment – A Status Report for Nepal: 2013/2014. Washington, DC: Government of Nepal and the Asia Foundation, 2014.

Larranaga, Osvaldo, Dante Contreras, and Jaime Ruiz-Tagle. Impact Evaluation of Chile Solidario: Lessons and Policy Recommendations. *Journal of Latin American Studies* 44 (2): 347–372, 2012.

McCrummen, Stephanie. "A Nigerian Neighborhood Symbolizes Nation's Tumble Toward Crisis," *Washington Post*, March 3, 2015, https://www.washingtonpost.com/world/africa/a-nigerian-neighborhood-symbolizes-nations-tumble-toward-crisis/2015/03/02/e5b28a16-b927-11e4-bc30-a4e75503948a_story.html

Maguire, Sheila, Joshua Freely, Carol Clymer, Maureen Conway, and Deena Schwartz. *Tuning into Local Labor Markets: Findings from the Sectoral Employment Study*. Washington, DC: Public/Private Ventures, July 2010.

Marquez Moscoso, Gustavo, and Cristobal Ruiz-Tagle. *Search Methods and Outcomes in Developing Countries: The Case of Venezuela*. Washington, DC: Inter-American Development Bank, IDB Research Department Working Paper Series No. 519, December 2004.

Mazza, Jacqueline. *Fast Tracking Jobs: Advances and Next Steps for Labor Intermediation Services in Latin America and the Caribbean*. Washington, DC: Inter-American Development Bank, IDB-TN-344, 2012.

———. *Estrategias Basados en Destrezas y Empleo: El Caso de Irlanda en Alto y Bajo Crecimiento*. Powerpoint Presentation at the Inter-American Development Bank, Washington, DC, February 2011.

———. Labour Intermediation Services: Lessons for Latin America and the Caribbean. *CEPAL Review* 80:159–167, August 2003.

———. *Unemployment Insurance: Case Studies and Lessons for Latin America and the Caribbean*. Washington, DC: Research Department, Inter-American Development Bank, Working Paper Series 411, October 1999.

Migration and Remittances Factbook 2011. Washington, DC: The World Bank, 2010.

Mourshed, M., D. Farrell, and D. Barton, *Education to Employment: Designing a System that Works*. Washington, DC: McKinsey Center for Government, 2012.

Nunn, Alex. Comments presented at Labor Intermediation Seminar: Performance Management in Public Employment Services. Washington, DC: Inter-American Development Bank, March 19, 2015.

Oya, Carlos. *Labor Market Policies: New Challenges Enhancing the Effectiveness of Active Labor Market Policies: A Streamlining Public Employment Service*. Paper Presented at Meeting of the Employment, Labour and Social Affairs Committee of the Ministerial Level held at the Chateau e la Muette, Paris on Tuesday 14 and Wednesday 15 October 1997, Paris, France, 1997.

Oya, Carlos, and Nicola Pontara. *Rural Wage Employment in Developing Countries*. Routledge ISS Studies in Rural Livelihoods. Hoboken: Taylor and Francis, 2015.

Paes-Souza, Romulo, Fernando Regalia, and Marco Stampini. *Conditions for Success in Implementing CCT Programs: Lessons for Asia from Latin America and the Caribbean*. Washington, DC: Inter-American Development Bank, Social Protection and Health Division, IDB-PB-192, 2013.

"Public Expenditure of LMP [labor market program] by main categories, % of GDP." in Organization of Economic Cooperation and Development (OECD) [database online]. Paris, France, 2013 [cited August/15 2015]. Available from http://stats.oecd.org/Index.aspx?DatasetCode=LMPEXP (accessed August 15, 2015.

Poetzsch, Johanna. *Case Management: The Magic Bullet for Labour Integration? An International Comparative Study*. Geneva, Switzerland: International Social Security Administration, Technical Report No. 6, 2008.

Productivity Brief 2015: Global Productivity Growth Stuck in the Slow Lane with no end in Sight. New York: The Conference Board, 2015.

"Public Expenditures of LMP [labor market policies] by main categories, % of GDP, 2013." Organization for Economic Cooperation and Development (OECD). Available from http://stats.oecd.org/Index.aspx?DatasetCode=LMPEXP

"*Resumen Ejecutivo*", in *El Mundo de los Servicios Publicos de Empleo*. Washington, DC: Asociación Mundial de los Servicios Públicos de Empleo (AMSPE); Banco Inter-Americano de Desarrollo (BID); Organización para la Cooperación y el Desarrollo Económico (OECD), 2015.

Ricart, Consuelo, Tzitzi Moran, and Christina Kappaz. *Toward a National Framework for Lifelong Learning in Mexico*. Washington, DC: Inter-American Development Bank, 2014.

Ridao-Cano, Cristobal, Rita Almeida, Sarojini Hirshleifer, David McKenzie, and A. Levent Yener. *Turkey: Evaluating the Impact of ISKUR's Vocational Training*. Washington D.C.: The World Bank, 82306 – TR, 2013.

Rodrik, Dani. Presentation at the Conference, "New Growth Strategies: Delivery on Their Promises", Washington, DC: The World Bank, October 14, 2014.

Rosenblum, Joshua L. *Looking for Work, Searching for Workers: American Labor Markets During Industrialization.* Cambridge: Cambridge University Press, 2002.

Scrivener, Susan, Johanna Walter, Tom Brock, and Gayle Hamilton. *National Evaluation of Welfare-To-Work Strategies: Evaluating Two Approaches to Case Management, Implementation, Participation Patterns, Costa and Three-Year Impacts of the Colombus Welfare-To-Work Program.* Washington, DC: Manpower Development Research Corporation, June 2001.

Sol, Els, and Mies Westerveld. *Contractualism in Employment Services: A New Form of Welfare Governance.* The Hague: Kluwer Law International, 2005

Søndergaard, Lars, Dina Abu-Ghaida, Christian Bodewig, Mamta Murthi, and Jan Rutkowski. *Skills, not Just Diplomas: Managing Education for Results in Eastern Europe and Central Asia.* Washington, D.C.: The World Bank, 2012.

South African Department of Higher Education and Training. *National Skills Development Strategy III.* Capetown, South Africa: South African Department of Higher Education and Training. 2012.

Swain, Ranjula Bali, and Adel Varghese. Delivery Mechanisms and Impact of Micro Finance Training in Indian Self-help Groups. *Journal of International Development* 25 (1): 11–21, January 2013.

Talent Shortage Survey: 2015. Milwaukee, WI: ManpowerGroup, 2015.

The Single Window Service in Asia and the Pacific: Piloting Integrated Approaches to Social Protection Floors. Geneva: International Labour Organization (ILO) Fact Sheet, 2014.

The State of Broadband 2015: Broadband as a Foundation for Sustainable Development. New York, NY: International Telecommunications Union (ITU), and United Nations Educational, Scientific and Cultural Organization (UNESCO), September 2015.

The World of Public Employment Services: Challenges, Capacity, and Outlook for Public Employment Services in the New World of Work. Washington, DC: Inter-American Development Bank, World Association of Public Employment Services, and the Organization of Economic Cooperation and Development, 2015.

Turkey: Evaluating the Impact of ISKUR's Vocational Training Programs. Washington, DC: The World Bank, Human Development Sector Unit, Europe and Central Asia Report, No. 82306-TR, August 2013.

UK Employment and Skills Almanac 2010. London, England: UK Commission on Employment and Skills, March 2011.

"Unemployment as a % of total labor force: 2012." In World Bank Jobs Databank. http://datatopics.worldbank.org/jobs/topic/employment

Vikstrom, Johan, Michael Rosholm, and Michael Svarer. *The Relative Efficiency of Active Labour Markeet Policy: Evidence from a Social Experiment and Non-Parametric Methods.* Uppsalla, Sweden: Institute for Labour Market Policy Evaluation, IFAU Working Paper 2011: 7, 2011.

"Vulnerable Employment as a Percentage of Total Employment: 2013." In World Bank Country Data, Labor Market Indicators. Washington, DC: The World Bank (accessed January 23, 2016).

Workforce Connections: Kenya Youth Assessment. Washington, DC: U.S. Agency for International Development, 2014.

"World Bank Country Classification by Income: 2016". World Bank [database online]. Washington, DC, 2015. http://data.worldbank.org/about/country-and-lending-groups (accessed October 10 2015).

World Development Report 2013: Jobs. Washington, DC: The World Bank, 2012.

World Economic Forum. *Matching Skills and Labor Market Needs, Building Social Partnerships for Better Skills and Better Jobs.* Davos, Switzerland: Davos-Klosters, January 2014.

World Employment and Social Outlook 2015. Geneva: International Labour Office (ILO), 2015.

World Urbanization Prospects: The 2014 Revision – Highlights. New York, NY: United Nations, Department of Economic and Social Affairs (UNDESA), United Nations Population Division, 2015.

"Youth Unemployment: 2013." In World Bank Jobs Databank, http://data.worldbank.org/indicator/SL.UEM.1524.ZS/countries/1W-4E-ZF-XQ-S3?display=graph. Washington, DC: The World Bank (accessed on September 15, 2015).

INDEX

A

active labor market policies, 1, 19, 20,
26, 27, 29, 32, 33, 35–7, 72, 73,
76, 95, 99, 110n3, 112n44, 114,
118, 134. (*See also under* specific
active labor market policies
training, employment services,
temporary employment programs,
wage subsidies)

Africa, 27, 59, 84, 92, 105, 129
public employment services,
27, 37, 72, 81

Africa, North. (*See also*
individual countries)
employment trends, 8
public employment services, 84

Alma Laurea, Italy, 107.
(*See also* higher education
information systems)

apprenticeships, 32, 34, 74, 120.
(*See also* training)

Arabian Peninsula, 77
immigration trends, 77

Argentina
integration of regional migrants,
116, 117, 119–23, 127–30

unemployment insurance
administration, 116, 125

Australia Jobs Network, 100

B

Bahamas, the
national employment
service, locational
issues, 51, 64n3
unemployment insurance
administration, 83

Benin public employment
service, 88

Betcherman, Gordon, 20, 34,
38n4, 110n4, 112n44

Brain Drain, (*See also* emigration,
highly educated brain drain)

Brazil
Ceara, regional non-profit
provider model, 43, 100
Galpão Aplauso, disadvantaged
youth training model, 75, 126
public employment service
and UI, 101

Bulgaria, 8, 13–15, 76

© The Author(s) 2017

J. Mazza, *Labor Intermediation Services in Developing Economies,*
DOI 10.1057/978-1-137-48668-4

C

Card, David, 38n2, 58, 110n3
career development services
   New Zealand, careersnz.com, 74
   United Kingdom Hospital
      Guild Career Program, 71
case management, 64n6, 66, 71,
   79, 85–8, 90–4, 97
Ceara, Brazil, regional non-profit
   model, 43, 100
Chile
   decentralized delivery
      of municipal employment
      services, 87
   labor market observatory, 70
   youth program, *Chile Joven,* 104
China
   employment trends, 11, 92
   migration patterns, 10
Colombia
   conditional cash transfer program,
      Jovenes en Accion, 125
   temporary agricultural migration
      program, 78
conditional and unconditional cash
   transfer programs, 85
*Consejo Hondureño de la Empresa
   Privada,* Honduran Council
   of the Private Sector, 44
core services, 24–7, 41, 43,
   46, 48, 51, 57, 58, 63, 64
Costa Rica, 4, 5, 11, 87
   decentralized delivery
      of employment
      services, 87
counselors, employment or job
   professionalization, training
      and development of
      (Stage 2), 90–3
   role in core services (Stage 1),
      24–5, 40–1

D

disadvantaged groups, considerations
   in employment/intermediation
   services, 68, 71, 74–6
discrimination, employment
   or labor market, 23, 27, 74
dismissal legislation, employment, 36
   impact on employment, 36
Dominican Republic, the
   public employment service, 58
   youth training program,
      Juventud y Empleo, 42, 66

E

East Asia, 9–11, 33, 34, 61,
   70, 74, 77, 110n12
   (*See also* Korea, Republic
      of; Malaysia; Singapore)
   employment response to financial
      crisis, 110n12
education, technical, 118, 120, 132
Egypt, 4, 9, 67, 72, 103, 105
   public employment agency, 72
El Salvador, 4, 5, 10, 11, 43, 46
   non-profit organization
      administration of national
      employment service, 43, 46
emigration, 10, 11, 77, 78.
   (*See also under* migration)
   highly educated (brain drain), 10
employment
   formal, 3, 6, 15, 23, 28, 44,
      46, 63, 73
   informal, 15, 118 (*see also*
      informality)
   social rationales for, 20–4
employment services
   core services of, 24–7, 41, 43,
      46, 48, 51, 57, 58, 63, 64
   definition, description, 24

impact evaluations and performance,
    20, 54 (*see also* Card, David;
    Kluve, Jochen)
international technical support,
    55–6
new institutional models (Stage 1),
    46 (*see also* labor
    intermediation services,
    institutional models,
    public-private-non-profit)
non-profit, 21, 26–8, 53
performance and monitoring
    indicators (Stage1), 53–6
private, 2, 3, 25, 26
public services/PES, 6, 27,
    30, 31, 37, 39, 42–4, 47,
    51, 53, 55, 56, 58, 61, 62,
    66, 67, 72, 75, 78–85, 87,
    88, 92, 94, 98–101, 109,
    112n45, 117, 122, 133,
    135n1 (*see also* public
    employment services PES)
rationale for, 20–4
entrepreneurship programs,
    81, 82, 111n23. (*See also*
    microenterprise programs;
    self-employment programs)
Estonia
    electronic platform, 126
    integration of social and labor
        programs, 92, 126

F
Fields, Gary, 8, 17n13
Finn, Dan, 37, 38, 96

G
Galpão Aplauso, 75, 126
Guatemala, 4, 5, 13, 78
    seasonal migration programs, 78

H
Haiti, 33, 43, 46, 74, 76
    temporary employment programs
        following 2010 earthquake, 33
higher education information systems,
    71. (*See also Alma Laurea*, Italy)
Honduras
    Council of the Private Sector,
        Honduran, 44, 45 (*see also
        Consejo Hondureño de la
        Empresa Privada*, Honduran
        Council of the Private Sector)
    public employment service,
        43, 44, 63
    public-private employment services
        network, 43, 101
human resources career
    development, 107–8
Hungary, 15, 35, 133

I
immigration, 10, 11, 77.
    (*See also under* migration)
impact evaluations
    employment services, 36
        (*see also* David Card
        and Jochen Kluve)
    entrepreneurship programs, 81, 85
    Mexico City public employment
        service, 20
    training programs, 54, 72, 75, 95
        (*see also* Card, David; Kluve,
        Jochen)
India
    microenterprise and women, 81
    skills mismatches, 13, 120, 132
informality, 2, 8, 23
information systems
    higher education, 71
        (*see also* higher education
        information systems)

information systems (*cont.*)
  labor market, 14, 21, 26,
    30, 31, 70, 105, 133 (*see also*
    observatories, labor market)
intake systems, computerized for job
  registry, 49–54
International Labour Organization
  (ILO), 8, 15, 26, 53, 55,
  126, 135n14
  Convention 197 on public-private
    intermediation services, 53
internet
  online job services using,
    60, 70, 71, 83
  usage rates among developing
    countries, 51, 89, 105
Ireland
  professionalization program for job
    counselors, 90–3, 108
  public employment service and
    integration of migrants,
    79, 102, 127
Italy, *Alma Laurea* university
  information system, 107.
  (*See also* higher education
  information systems)

J
Jamaica, 47, 82, 101, 102
  electronic labor exchange
    (ELE), public
    employment service, 102
job banks or registries, 21, 24,
  26, 40, 45, 71, 77, 78, 102.
  (*See also* employment services,
  core services)
  computerized intake systems,
    49–54 (*see also* intake systems,
    computerized for job registry)
job fairs, 24, 51, 54, 57, 60, 76, 77,
  95, 102, 126

job search
  assistance services, 83
  costs and time in, 21–2, 42
  counseling services, 24–5, 26, 40–1
  formal methods, 3, 6, 14
  informal or "family and friends"
    methods, 3–6
  information barriers to, 21
  studies on, 1, 104
Jordan
  public employment service, 72
  wage subsidies, 73
Jovenes Youth Training Model, 125.
  (*See also* youth)

K
Kluve, Jochen, 38n6, 58, 110n3
Korea, Republic of
  employment crisis, 1982, 61–2
  employment information service
    (KEIS), 104
  public employment service, 62

L
labor force participation
    in developing economies
  adult,
  youth, 9
labor intermediation services
  case management by, 90
  definition of, 20, 32
  extended services of; information
    services (Type 1), 68–71, 86,
    102; intermediation "plus"
    services (Type 2), 68, 86, 102;
    program administration-support
    (Type 3), 68–9, 86, 102
  impact evaluations of employment
    services, 95 (*see also* Card,
    David; and Kluve, Jochen)

institutional models, public-private-non-profit, 44
job promoters (business liaisons), 50, 89
one-stop service models, 87, 93
on-line service delivery, 52, 87, 88, 91, 92 (*see also* internet)
performance and monitoring indicators (Stage 2), 53–4
program administration, 30–2, 84–5
social services administration, 123–6
labor market observatories, 70
Latin America and the Caribbean, 3–5, 11, 37, 43, 55, 56, 58, 72, 110n11, 111n22, 111n30
Regional Network of Public Employment Services (Red SEALC), 55, 56
Lebanon
employment trends, 23, 72
public employment agency, 72, 101
Legal-Regulatory Issues for Employment and Labor Intermediation Services,

M
Macedonia, 36, 48
youth employment centers, 48
Malaysia, 106, 127–9
national skills strategy, 106
management reforms. (*See also* specific reform types)
case management, 90–4
co-location of services, 93–4
monitoring and evaluation, 94–8
one-stop shops, 93, 94
professionalization and training of job counselors, 90–3
single window service, 126
Manpower Group, 2, 13, 14, 136n28
Mexico

labor market observatory, 102 (*see also* labor market observatories)
portal del empleo, 102
responses to employment crises, 35
Riviera Maya public-private partnership, 73, 109, 121–3 (*see also* Riviera Maya public-private partnership for tourism)
seasonal migration programs, 78
servicio nacional del empleo (SNE), 43
microenterprise programs, 71, 80. (*See also* self-employment)
Middle East. (*See also under* individual countries)
employment trends, 66
private employment agencies for low-skilled migrants, 77
public employment services, 67, 72, 81
migration
"brain drain" from developing countries,
economic (for work), 10–12
internal, 77, 78
private agencies for, 79
return migration programs, Tonga example, 131
support services, 10, 12, 26, 29, 77, 102
trends in developing countries, 10–11
Ministries of Labor
labor inspection, regulatory offices, 51
and public employment services, 53
mobility, labor, 77, 78, 118
promoting internal, 118
monitoring and evaluation, 54, 72, 74, 86, 87, 94, 95

Morocco
   public employment service, 103
   wage subsidies, 73–4
M-Pesa mobile payment network, 105

N

Neither Employed, in Education
   or in Training (NEET).
   (*See* youth, idle or discouraged)
Nepal, Foreign employment exchange
   board, 70

O

observatories, labor market.
   (*See also* portals, employment)
   Poland, 7
   Syria, 70
one-stop service centers, 87
online job services
   Caribbeanjobs.com, 27, 40
   Monster.com, 2, 27
Organization for Economic
   Cooperation and Development
   (OECD), 35–7, 38n16, 40, 42,
   43, 56, 88, 93, 96, 100, 105,
   112n47

P

Panama, 4, 5
Paraguay, 4, 5, 80, 88, 111n21
passive labor market policies,
   32, 35, 116. (*See also*
   unemployment insurance)
performance and monitoring
   indicators
   for stage 1, employment
      services, 39–64, 88
      (*see also* employment services)
   for stage 2, labor intermediation
      services, 65–112

Peru, 4, 5, 13, 27, 76, 94, 132
   single window service, 94
placement, job, 20, 24–30, 33, 39, 41,
   42, 47, 57–9, 64n5, 67, 72–5,
   83, 84, 87, 95, 96, 98, 104, 106,
   118, 122. (*See also* core services;
   employment services)
specialized placement for
   employers, 82
Poland, 71, 77, 79, 116
   labor market observatory, 71
portals, employment, 69–71. (*See also*
   observatories, labor market)
portal de empleo, Mexico, 102
program administration by labor
   intermediation services, 30, 31,
   83, 84
public employment services (PES).
   (*See also under* individual countries)
   Middle East and North Africa, 16n2
   networks, 55
   *Red de Servicios de Empleo de
      America Latina y el Caribe*
      (Red SEALC), 55, 56
   World Association of Public
      Employment Services
      (WAPES), 55, 56

R

*Red de Servicios de Empleo de America
   Latina y el Caribe* (Red SEALC),
   55, 56. (*See also* public
   employment services (PES),
   networks)
Riviera Maya public-private
   partnership for tourism, 121–2
Rodrik, Dani, 128, 129, 135n24
Romania, 14, 106
   employment trends, 14
rural, adaptations for employment/
   intermediation services, 60–1
Russia, 8, 15, 59, 77

S

self-employment programs, 30, 80, 124, 125. (*See also* microenterprise programs)
Singapore, 13, 59, 92, 106, 127–9
national skills strategy, 106
single window service delivery, 126, 135n14. (*See also* management reforms)
skills
advancing skill content of work, 131–4
deficits in workforce, 72, 74
mismatches, 2, 13, 14, 23–4, 28, 120, 131, 132
social assistance, 16, 31, 32, 85, 94, 98, 124, 125
coordination with the delivery of employment/intermediation services, 16, 94
social service administration-gateway by labor intermediation services, 85–6
South Africa
skills development strategy, 76, 121
youth build project, 76
Switzerland, 31, 84, 96, 101
public employment service and UI delivery, 31, 84
Syria
labor market observatory, 70
public employment service, 72

T

Ta3mal network, 105
temporary employment programs, 33
training and programs
apprenticeships, 32, 34, 120
impact evaluations, 20, 54, 72, 95
(*see also* Card, David; and Kluve, Jochen)

microenterprise, 71, 81, 91, 102
youth, 42, 58, 66, 75, 125
Tunisia
prohibition against private employment services, 53
public employment service, 87
wage subsidies, 73–4
Turkey, 9, 11, 13, 31, 72, 73, 78, 83, 85, 100, 107, 110n8, 120
ISKUR, public employment agency, 72, 73, 85

U

Ukraine, 10, 11, 77, 78, 110n17
labor market information, 78
unemployment, 3, 7, 8, 14, 17n11, 22, 26, 31–7, 38n13, 42, 61, 62, 65, 83–5, 92–4, 96–8, 101, 102, 111n30, 112n47, 116, 125, 126, 130
unemployment insurance, 3, 26, 31, 32, 35, 36, 42, 61, 65, 83–5, 92, 94, 98, 101, 102, 111n38, 112n47, 125, 126, 135n15
administration by public employment services, 26, 31, 42, 83–5
(*see also* Switzerland)
United Kingdom
hospital guild, career development program, 71
Job Centre Plus Employment Centers,
"One" service integration, 94
U.S. Agency for International Development (USAID), Workforce Development Group, 55

V

Vietnam public employment service, 88
volatility, job or employment, 19, 22
vulnerable employment, 8, 9

W

wage subsidies, 29, 33, 34, 73, 125
workforce development, 55, 109,
    119–21, 128
World Association of Public
    Employment Services (WAPES),
    55, 56. (*See also* public employment
    services (PES), networks)
World Bank, 9, 13, 20, 55, 73, 78, 81,
    86, 103, 110n13, 116, 131, 132,
    136n25

Y

Yemen, 4, 102
youth
    idle or discouraged, 9–10
    labor force participation,
        9, 10
    Latin American *Jovenes*
        model, 125
    neither employed, nor
        in education or training
        (NEET),
    specialized youth employment
        interventions, 7 (*see also*
        Youth Build International)
    training Models, 58
    unemployment, 8, 116
Youth Build International, 76